The TV Tidbits
Classic Television
Trivia Quiz Book

Also by Craig Hamrick:

Big Lou: the Life and Career of Actor Louis Edmonds
Barnabas & Company: the Cast of the TV Classic Dark Shadows
The Dark Shadows Collector's Guide
The Dark Shadows Collectibles Book

Hamrick also wrote the preface to *The Power of Halloween* by Diana Millay, and his photography is featured in the vampire novel *Kiss Me Kill Me* by Michael Karol

The TV Tidbits Classic Television Trivia Quiz Book

Craig Hamrick

iUniverse, Inc.
New York Lincoln Shanghai

The TV Tidbits Classic Television Trivia Quiz Book

iUniverse, Inc.

For information address:
iUniverse, Inc.
2021 Pine Lake Road, Suite 100
Lincoln, NE 68512
www.iuniverse.com

Cover art images: © www.clipart.com

ISBN: 0-595-31034-6

Printed in the United States of America

For my favorite classic TV stars, the special ladies of *Dark Shadows*, whose support during my battle with colon cancer has meant more than I can say:
Nancy Barrett, Diana Millay, Lara Parker, Kathryn Leigh Scott, and Marie Wallace.

Contents

Acknowledgements

Special Thanks to: My editor and great friend, Michael Karol; and to my boyfriend, Joe Salvatore, for watching hours of television with me.

Introduction

My earliest encounter with a classic TV star happened in a Kansas trailer park in the early 1970s. But it wasn't as tawdry as that might sound. I was a starry eyed kid who loved television, and one of my favorite shows was the campy *Batman*, and Robin, the Boy Wonder, visited my hometown when I was about six years old.

I was so young that I didn't quite understood yet that it wasn't actually Robin, but a young actor named Burt Ward, who was working his way across the U.S. making personal appearances. My big brother Mark and I were excited from the moment we saw an ad in the newspaper announcing that the superhero would be signing autographs at a mobile home dealership in Coffeyville.

Mark was six years older, so he was a bit shrewder than me. He realized we were about to get a once-in-a-lifetime chance. He figured out that while we were getting our autographs we'd each have a moment to ask Robin one question. So, for days we planned, debating exactly what we'd inquire about. I don't remember what questions we passed over, but I vividly recall the two we settled on: Mark wanted to know how Batman and Robin were able to pull large items, like a big can of shark repellant, from their relatively small utility belts. And I would ask which super villain was Robin's favorite. (I was sure I already knew the answer. I imagined that, like me, he had a special place in his heart for slinky, amazingly costumed Catwoman, but I wanted to know for sure.)

The exciting Bat-day arrived, and our father drove us to the trailer park. Dad didn't grasp the size of the moment. It was a balmy afternoon. He preferred to wait in the air-conditioned car while Mark and I took our place in a line that started inside a luxurious double-wide and snaked its way among a half a dozen mobile homes. And it wasn't made up just of children. There were also a few farmers in from the field, in their mud-stained overalls; housewives with big, teased hair; and even a couple of local businessmen in their pinstriped suits. (Coffeyville didn't see many celebrities, so when one showed up, people turned out.)

"What are you going to ask him?" Mark asked me as we stood there sweating. He was afraid that in the excitement I'd forget or just stand there tongue-tied. But I remembered my question, and I recited it belligerently to him. "I'm *not* going to forget," I said. But just in case, I did keep repeating it over and over in my head.

Finally we made our way into the magic trailer—and there, sitting behind a desk, was Robin. I was used to seeing the show on our black-and-white TV set, so his bright red vest and shiny yellow satin cape looked intense. And even with that little bandit mask concealing part of his face, I could tell he'd aged a bit since the TV show was made.

There were still a few people ahead of us, so we got to watch Robin in action. He had a stack of black-and-white photos in front of him, and as each kid approached, he asked their name, and with a magic marker grasped in his green-gloved hand, he signed a personalized autograph. I was a little smug when I noticed that nobody else was asking questions. (Unlike most people living in Coffeyville, Mark and I weren't born there. This was just another example of how our big-city ways set us apart from the natives.)

Mark was in front of me, so he got his superhero moment first. When Robin snapped, "Name?!" Mark told him, and he kept his cool under pressure; he also asked his question: "How did you and Batman fit all those gadgets into your utility belts?" Robin didn't miss a beat: "They were really big belts! Next!"

As Mark moved aside, still glowing a bit from his experience, I stepped up. I was soft-spoken, so after Robin asked my name and I told him, he yelled over his shoulder, to no one in particular, "Is it Craig or Greg!?" There were a few people milling about behind him—probably the owner of the trailer park and his proud family. Maybe Robin thought my parents were in the trailer somewhere, but Dad was out in the car, and Mark had moved on, so I was on my own. I spoke up and told him my name again. Then as he scribbled it on a photo for me, I asked my question: "Which villain was your favorite?" He didn't even think about it. "I hated 'em all," he said blithely. Before I knew it, our audience with Robin was over, and we hadn't really learned a thing.

I didn't know it then, but what my brother and I were seeking that day was TV trivia. We were going right to the source; we wanted Batman's trusty chum to tell us some little-known facts about one of our favorite shows. And even though Robin didn't really give up the goods, for me, it was the beginning of a life-long interest in the details that made up the fabulous worlds depicted on our family TV screen.

When I wasn't watching TV, I spent a lot of happy hours reading about it—everything from paperbacks and comic books based on popular shows (like *The Partridge Family* and *Dark Shadows*) to magazines that offered gossip about the stars and previews of episodes to come. One of my favorite magazines was

Dynamite, which was aimed at kids like me and which included posters of everyone from John Travolta to Farrah Fawcett-Majors. I covered my bedroom walls with those posters, and I filled my mind with as much trivial information about my favorite shows as I could find.

As I grew up, my love for TV shows only intensified. Over the years I've interviewed dozens of actors, including classic TV stars like Carol Burnett, Stefanie Powers, Conrad Bain, and Jonathan Frid. For various writing projects, I've spent hundreds of hours conducting extensive research at the New York Public Library for the Performing Arts and the Museum of Television and Radio. And as opposed to the half-dozen channels the antenna on our TV captured when I was a kid, today I have digital cable, with more than 200 channels, plus a collection of classics on VHS and DVD.

Along with my friend Michael Karol, another writer who loves TV as much as I do, I've started the TV Tidbits book series and website. To prepare this Tidbits volume of trivia quizzes, I re-watched countless episodes of my favorite shows, pored through reference books and magazine and newspaper articles, and spent hours surfing the Web. It was certainly a labor of love, and if you're a TV fan like me, I think you'll enjoy the challenge of working your way through the pages. Stay tuned for more in the Tidbits book series and visit www.tvtidbits.com to read fun facts about your favorite shows.

Craig Hamrick
February 2004

PART I
The Big Quiz

◆

200 Questions about TV Favorites

Classic Shows

1. What sitcom's theme song started out, "Come and knock on our door..."?

2. What was the name of the newspaper where *Lou Grant* worked?

3. What did U.N.C.L.E. stand for, on *The Man from U.N.C.L.E.*?

4. What type of business did the girls run on the *Golden Girls* spin-off *The Golden Palace*?

5. How was Carla's husband, Eddie LeBec, killed on *Cheers*?

6. What was the name of the super-intelligent pig on *Green Acres*?

7. What sitcom featured Tom Hanks as a cross-dresser?

8. What part of her body did Carol Burnett tug, at the end of each *Carol Burnett Show* episode?

9. What hugely influential variety show was broadcast from the theater later taken over by *Late Night with David Letterman*?

10. What show did *The Facts of Life* spin-off from?

11. Who was the building superintendent on *One Day at a Time*?

12. Who was the host of *Fantasy Island*?

13. What kind of animal was *Gentle Ben*?

14. What former Miss America played *Barnaby Jones*' assistant?

15. Who was *Trapper John, M.D.*'s sidekick?

16. What was the name of the hotel featured on *Hotel*?

17. What was the name of *The Love Boat*?

18. Which title character of *Holmes and Yoyo* was a robot? Who played the two title characters?

19. What was Nurse Gloria Brancusi's nickname on *Trapper John, M.D.*?

20. What kind of car did *Magnum, P.I* drive?

21. Name the three Lawrence children on *Family*.

22. What character did John Ritter play on *The Waltons*?

23. Who played the crime-fighting brothers *The Hardy Boys*?

24. What race of robots did Starbuck and Apollo battle on *Battlestar Galactica*?

25. What kind of candy did *Kojak* constantly suck on?

26. What were the first names of Grandma and Grandpa on *The Waltons*?

27. What was the name of Laura Ingalls' bratty nemesis on *The Little House on the Prairie*?

28. What type of dwelling did Jim Rockford live in, on *The Rockford Files*?

29. Before *Baywatch*, what daytime soap opera role did David Hasselhoff play?

30. Who played Sally, the "wife" half of *McMillan and Wife*, opposite Rock Hudson?

31. Who wrote the book that inspired *Please Don't Eat the Daisies*?

32. What type of colorfully painted vehicle did Shirley pilot on *The Partridge Family*?

33. What was the name of the Duke boys' car on *The Dukes of Hazzard*?

34. What nighttime soap starred Ryan O'Neal, Mia Farrow, and Ruth Warrick?

35. What kind of pet did *Baretta* have?

36. How many daughters did Ann have on *One Day at a Time*?

37. What comic strip character did Jay North play?

38. What former *Saturday Night Live* star played the title character in *Scrooged*, the 1988 remake of *A Christmas Carol*?

39. What was the title of *Saturday Night Live* alum Gilda Radner's memoir about the early stages of her battle with cancer? (Hint: She used one of her Roseanne Roseannadanna catchphrases.)

40. What actress guest-starred as Lucy's eccentric librarian roommate on *The Lucy Show*?

41. Why did Jamie Sommers require bionic parts on *The Bionic Woman*? Which of Jamie's body parts were bionic?

42. What was the name of the doctor who supervised the bionic functions of *The Bionic Woman* and *The Six Million Dollar Man*?

43. What was Steve Austin's job before he became *The Six Million Dollar Man*?

44. Name the hospital on *Emergency!*

45. *The Golden Girls*' neighbors got their own spin-off in 1988. Name it.

46. Who was *Maude*'s maid, later spun-off into her own sitcom?

47. Which character from *The Jeffersons* was spun-off into her own very short-lived series, *Checking In*?

48. On *The Jeffersons*, what type of business did George Jefferson own? What was George's nickname for his wife, Louise?

49. What real-life U.S. Vice President publicly criticized *Murphy Brown*'s title character for being an unwed mother?

50. What was the occupation of Donna's husband on *The Donna Reed Show*?

51. Which *Hollywood Squares* regular was also a frequent guest star on *Donny and Marie*?

52. On what late-night talk show did Arnold Schwarzenegger announce his candidacy for the office of governor of California?

53. On *Moonlighting*, what was the name of the detective agency? How did it get that name?

54. Who proposed to Maddie just before she and David "hit the sheets" for the first time on *Moonlighting*? What was the character's claim to fame?

55. What was the name of Buck's robot sidekick on *Buck Rogers in the 25th Century*?

56. How did the final episode of *Benson* end?

57. What was J.J.'s explosive catchphrase on *Good Times*? What future pop singing sensation played Penny on the show?

58. What section of New York was the setting for *Barney Miller*?

59. How did each episode of *Mork & Mindy* end?

60. What storybook characters were the two main characters of *The Charmings*?

61. What had happened to Julia's husband before the first episode of *Julia*?

62. Name the fort featured on *F Troop*.

63. What does "ALF" stand for, on *ALF*?

64. What happened at the end of the final episode of *Newhart*?

65. Which U.S. president was James T. West's boss on *The Wild Wild West*?

66. What was the collective nickname of Gabe's students on *Welcome Back, Kotter*?

67. What kind of car did Dan Tanna drive on *Vegas*?

68. Whose murder investigation was the subject of the early episodes of *Twin Peaks*?

69. Who played Henry's nagging mother-in-law on *Too Close For Comfort*?

70. Which singer was Judge Harry Stone obsessed with, on *Night Court*?

71. Name *The Green Hornet*'s car.

72. Name Sgt. Carter's girlfriend on *Gomer Pyle, U.S.M.C.*

73. What type of doctor did Gloria work for on the *All in the Family* spin-off *Gloria*? What former *Batman* villain played the doctor?

74. How were *Charlie's Angels* Jill and Kris Munroe related?

75. What sport did Jill leave the detective business to pursue, on *Charlie's Angels*?

76. Where was Max Smart's secret phone hidden, on *Get Smart*?

77. On *The Flip Wilson Show*, Flip often donned a wig and dress to portray a sassy female character. Name her.

78. Which one of Ben Cartwright's sons had to be written out of *Bonanza* when the actor who played the character died? Name the actor.

79. What newspaper did Tim O'Hara work for on *My Favorite Martian*?

80. On *My Favorite Martian*, when the Martian moved in with him, who did Tim tell his friends the alien was?

81. What sitcom starred Marlo Thomas as an aspiring actress with a boyfriend named Donald and an exasperated dad named Lou played by an actor named Lew?

82. What 1968–70 romantic comedy featured a unique romance between the ghost of a sea captain and a living lady who shared a house called Gull Cottage?

83. What was unusual about the character Jennifer on *Jennifer Slept Here*?

84. What 1989–98 sitcom featured a nerdy young character named Urkel?

85. What was the name of Tim's TV show-within-a-show on *Home Improvement*?

86. Who sang the theme song for *Chico and the Man*?

87. Why was Chico written out of *Chico and the Man*?

88. What was Kramer's first name on *Seinfeld*? What type of book did he go on *Live! With Regis and Kathy Lee* to promote?

89. Who played the title thief in *It Takes a Thief*? What dance legend joined the cast in 1969 as his father, also a master thief?

90. Why did Peter marry Dora on *I Married Dora*?

91. Which title character was blond on *Starsky and Hutch*?

92. Lucille Ball was such a big fan of a 1970s comedy classic that she hosted a special two-part retrospective. What was the series?

93. *Buffy the Vampire Slayer* fell in love with two bloodsuckers. Name them.

94. What dramatic film was this comedy series *Alice* based on? One actor and one actress from the film were part of the TV cast of *Alice*. Name them and their characters.

95. What was Flo's catchphrase on *Alice*?

96. In the somber final moments of the last episode of *Roseanne*, it was revealed that recent, bizarre episodes had been Roseanne's fantasies, and one of the main characters had died. Who passed away?

97. In 1975, David McCallum starred in a short-lived, modern update of a 1933 Claude Rains film about a doctor with a special physical quality. Name the show.

98. Who got the Dear John letter on *Dear John*?

99. What catastrophic event happened in the first episode of *Space: 1999*?

100. Who provided the voice for the mother/car on *My Mother the Car*?

101. Which Duke from *The Dukes of Hazzard* played the title character's ex-husband on Cybill Shepherd's sitcom *Cybill*?

102. What was the title character's big announcement about her lifestyle in a groundbreaking 1997 episode of Ellen DeGeneres' *Ellen*?

103. Which character on *The Bob Newhart Show* was a grownup orphan?

104. On *Logan's Run*, what type of vehicle did Logan and Jessica use? What was the name of their robot companion?

105. What actor starred in four of the five original *The Planet of the Apes* films and on the TV series?

106. What was the name of Caroline's cat on *Caroline in the City*?

107. Which former *Star Trek* science officer hosted the documentary series *In Search Of…*?

108. Which war was the backdrop of Ron Harper's 1967–68 drama *Garrison's Gorillas*?

109. What childhood trauma compelled Fox Mulder to investigate unusual phenomena on *The X-Files*?

110. Which sitcom did First Lady Nancy Regan visit to promote her "Just Say No" anti-drug message?

111. Who took over David Janssen's role as *The Fugitive* Richard Kimble when the 1963–67 series was remade in 2000?

112. What sport was the specialty of *Phenom* Angela Doolan?

113. What disease plagued Lily's aging mom on *Once and Again*?

114. Who played the title characters of *The Mothers-in-Law*?

115. Who provided the voice of Miss Piggy on *The Muppet Show*?

Golden Oldies

116. Who played *My Little Margie* (1952–55)? In what city did Margie and her father, Vern, live?

117. Which of the future *Golden Girls* starred in *Date With the Angels* (1957–58)? What did Mr. Angel do for a living?

118. Successful film comedienne Joan Davis played the wacky wife of a judge played by future *Gilligan's Island* millionaire Jim Backus, from 1952 to '55. Name the series, and name Joan and Jim's characters.

119. In 1960, the next-door neighbor of the title character of *December Bride* (1954–61), was spun-off into his own series, starring Harry Morgan. Name the spin-off.

120. Film stars (and real-life spouses) Ida Lupino and Howard Duff played a married couple in a 1957 to '58 comedy. Name the show and the occupations of the two main characters.

121. Lucille Ball's 1948 radio show *My Favorite Husband* made it to TV in the 1950s without Lucille. Who took over her leading role, as Liz? What was the occupation of Liz's husband?

122. Which of Ozzie and Harriet Nelson's sons became a pop singing star on *The Adventures of Ozzie & Harriet*?

123. What breed of dog was featured in *The Adventures of Rin Tin Tin*? What was the name of his human pal?

124. Who played Ellie Banks, mother of the bride, in the series *Father of the Bride*? (Joan Bennett played the part in the film of the same name.)

125. Another curvaceous blonde took over the part originated by Marilyn Monroe in the 1957 to '59 series based on the film *How to Marry a Millionaire*. Name the actress and the character.

126. Before he played lazybones Uncle Joe on *Petticoat Junction*, Edgar Buchanan was a little more active as *Hopalong Cassidy*'s sidekick, from 1952 to '53. Name his character.

Game Shows

127. In more-tasteful times (the 1970s), what musical-sounding word did Brett Somers and her fellow *Match Game* panelists use instead of "urinate"?

128. What phrase does the announcer call out to encourage contestants to come from the audience and join the game on *The Price is Right*?

129. Which game show did movie star Burt Reynolds help invent, based on a game he and his pals had perfected in his home?

130. What perpetually youthful host presided over *$100,000 Pyramid*?

131. Who was the most famous letter-turner on *Wheel of Fortune*?

132. What type of Las Vegas gambling machine did contestants play with on *The Joker's Wild*?

133. What female psychologist capitalized on her knowledge about boxing to take the grand prize on *The $64,000 Question*?

134. Who was the initial host of *Who Wants to Be a Millionaire*? Who took over for the syndicated daytime version?

135. Which show did a harsh-demeanored, leather-clad Anne Robinson host?

136. What happened when contestants said "the secret word" on Groucho Marx's 1950s game show *You Bet Your Life*?

137. What movie star occupied the center square for the first several years in the syndicated revival of *Hollywood Squares*, beginning in 1998?

Short-Lived Shows

138. What was *The Girl With Something Extra*'s special talent? Who played her, and who played her husband?

139. Which one of the future *Friends* played Ferris Bueller's sister on the TV series based on the popular movie *Ferris Bueller's Day Off*?

140. On *Paper Moon*, who took over the role Tatum O'Neal played in the film?

141. Where was *Dirty Dancing* set? Who played Johnny Castle?

142. For three months in 1978, former Miss America Phyllis George hosted a show based on (and named after) a popular celebrity-focused magazine. Name it.

143. Patty Duke played the first female U.S. president on a sitcom that aired for a few months in 1985. What was the name of the show, and who played her husband?

144. So far, all of the principal cast members from *Seinfeld* who have tried headlining their own sitcoms have gone down in flames. Jason Alexander's attempt as a self-help guru lasted less than a month. Name the series.

145. Former *Dark Shadows* star Kathryn Leigh Scott (Maggie Evans) played the assistant manager of an Atlantic City casino on a series that aired on CBS from September to October 1979. Name the series and the casino.

146. If *That 70s Show* was a smash hit, wouldn't another decade fare just as well? Um…no. Name the failed series that tried to follow in *70s'* footsteps.

147. Even the most brilliant comic ever to grace the small screen had a misfire. Name Lucille Ball's only TV flop, which lasted a couple of months in 1986.

148. Without her bionic super powers, Lindsay Wagner had a little more trouble headlining a show; *Jesse* ran from September to November 1984. What was the occupation of her title character, Jesse?

149. Which former *Saturday Night Live* star hosted perhaps the worst (and certainly one of the most-quickly cancelled) talk shows in the history of television?

Costumed Superheroes

150. On *Batman*, to downplay any sexual impropriety that viewers might have read into the situation of bachelors Bruce Wayne and Dick Grayson sharing Bruce's stately mansion, a female character was invented to live with them. Name this lady, who was not part of *Batman's* comic book world—and what was her relation to Bruce?

151. Name the three purrrrrr-fect actresses who played Catwoman on the TV series *Batman* and the film based on it.

152. At the height of its popularity in 1966, how many nights per week did *Batman* air?

153. In what city did *The Flash* take place? Who played the fleet-footed title character?

154. On the Saturday-morning cartoon *Superfriends,* what was the name of the building where the superhero team met? Who melodramatically narrated the series?

155. What was unusual about *Wonder Woman's* plane?

156. What special purpose did *Wonder Woman's* bracelets serve?

157. In what magazine did Lyle Waggoner, who played *Wonder Woman*'s boy-friend Steve Trevor, pose nude in the 1970s?

158. What future movie star had a recurring role on *Wonder Woman* as Wonder Girl?

159. What was the name of the young man who cried out, "Shazam!" in order to transform himself into Captain Marvel, on *Shazam*?

160. How did archeologist Andrea Thomas turn herself into *Isis*?

161. What iconic singer was Perry White's favorite, on *Lois and Clark*?

162. What color was *The Incredible Hulk*?

163. What supernatural soap star played David Banner's doomed wife on the first episode of *The Incredible Hulk*?

164. Which Elvis Presley movie featured Yvonne Craig as one of the love interests, a couple of years before she played Batgirl on *Batman*?

165. What bumbling superhero was the main character of the British sitcom *My Hero*?

166. What event gave Peter Parker the special powers of *The Amazing Spiderman*?

167. When John Hinckley tried to kill President Ronald Regan in real life, the name of the leading character of a 1981–83 superhero show was quickly changed from Hinkley to Hanley. Name the show and the Robert Redford-look-alike actor who played Hinkley/Hanley.

168. Buck Henry (co-creator of *Get Smart*) created a superhero parody series in 1967, starring William Daniels as the hero and Alice Ghostley as his nagging mother. Name the sitcom.

169. The Saturday morning kids' show *Electrawoman and Dynagirl* starred one of daytime's most enduring soap stars as Electrawoman. Name the actress and her *Days of Our Lives* character.

The 1990s and Beyond

170. What was the name of the coffee house where the *Friends* hung out?

171. Which of the President's daughters was kidnapped in 2003 on *The West Wing*?

172. What major purchase did the President's secretary, Mrs. Landingham, make just before her death on *The West Wing*. How did she die?

173. What former child star guest-starred as Karen's divorce lawyer on *Will & Grace*?

174. What did Jack call his cabaret show on *Will & Grace*?

175. What type of homicides did Lily work on, on *Cold Case*?

176. What talent-seeking show featured a less-than-polite British judge named Simon, along with pop singer Paula Abdul?

177. What does *JAG* stand for?

178. How many gay men worked their magic on heterosexuals on *Queer Eye for the Straight Guy*?

179. The ghost of which sitcom legend visited Lisa when she tried to run the household in her mom's absence, on *The Simpsons*?

180. On *The Simpsons*, Bart and Lisa's favorite TV show was the cartoon *Itchy and Scratchy*. What kind of animals are Itchy and Scratchy?

181. What former *Days and Nights of Molly Dodd* star showed up claiming to be Clark Kent's biological mom on *Smallville*?

182. Which *Star Trek* spin-off featured former *Quantum Leap* star Scott Bakula as the captain of the Enterprise?

183. What MTV series about seven strangers who are forced to live together and have their lives taped, kicked off a reality programming craze?

184. What does SVU stand for on the show *Law & Order: SVU*?

185. What legendary movie star was the mother of *SVU* star Mariska Hargitay?

186. Name the Crane brothers' coffee house hangout on *Fraiser*.

187. How did Daphne first become acquainted with the Crane family on *Fraiser*?

188. What was Mavis' claim to fame on *Whoopi*?

189. What *8 Simple Rules for Dating My Teenage Daughter* star's death was written into the show's storyline?

190. Which *Law & Order* detective, played by a Broadway veteran, couldn't resist making bad jokes while investigating homicides?

191. Who was the first winner on *Survivor*?

192. Which actor was the first of many to bare his behind on *NYPD Blue*?

193. What former star of daytime soap *All My Children* and nighttime drama *NYPD Blue* was briefly a cast member of *CSI: Miami*?

194. How did *Law & Order: SVU*'s sexy Assistant D.A. Alexandra Cabot exit the show in 2003?

195. Which over-the-top reality game show forces participants to eat creepy things like worms?

196. What was *Judge Judy*'s last name?

197. How did Dr. Romano die on *ER*?

198. What film star guest-starred on several episodes of *The Practice* as an attorney who claims to hear messages from God?

199. Which of the *South Park* kids was Jewish?

200. What pampered society girls briefly moved to Arkansas to star on the 2004 reality show *The Simple Life*?

Big Quiz—Answers

1. *Three's Company*
2. *The Los Angeles Tribune*
3. United Network Command for Law Enforcement
4. A hotel
5. The hockey star was run over on the ice by a Zamboni.
6. Arnold
7. *Bosom Buddies*
8. Her ear
9. *The Ed Sullivan Show*
10. *Diff'rent Strokes*
11. Duane Schneider
12. Mr. Roarke
13. A black bear
14. Lee Meriwether
15. Gonzo Gates
16. The St. Gregory
17. The Pacific Princess
18. Yoyo (John Schuck) was the robot. Richard B. Shull played Holmes.
19. Ripples
20. A Ferrari
21. Buddy (Kristy MacNichol), Nancy (Meredith Baxter Birney), and Willie (Gary Frank)
22. Rev. Matthew Fordwick
23. Parker Stevenson and Shawn Cassidy
24. Cylons
25. A lollipop
26. Zeb and Esther
27. Nellie Oleson
28. A trailer
29. Snapper on *The Young and the Restless*
30. Susan Saint James
31. Jean Kerr
32. An old school bus
33. The General Lee
34. *Peyton Place*
35. A cockatoo

36. Two—Julie and Barbara
37. *Dennis the Menace*
38. Bill Murray
39. *It's Always Something*
40. Carol Burnett
41. A skydiving accident left her body badly battered. Both legs, an arm, and one ear were all made bionic.
42. Dr. Rudy Wells
43. Astronaut
44. Rampart Hospital
45. *Empty Nest*
46. Florida Evans became the main character of *Good Times*.
47. The Jeffersons' maid, Florence
48. A chain of dry-cleaning stores, Weezy
49. Dan Quayle
50. He's a pediatrician.
51. Paul Lynde
52. *The Tonight Show with Jay Leno*
53. David renamed the agency Blue Moon Detective Agency in honor of the shampoo Maddie used to endorse. (She was known as "the Blue Moon girl.")
54. Sam, a former astronaut
55. Twiki, voiced by Mel Blanc (best known for voicing Bugs Bunny)
56. Benson and Governor Gatling were watching election returns; they were running against each other for the office of governor. The winner was not revealed.
57. Dyn-o-mite!; Janet Jackson
58. Barney's squad room was located in Greenwich Village.
59. Mork reported in to his boss, Orson.
60. The show featured Prince Charming and Snow White living in the 1980s.
61. He was killed in the Vietnam War.
62. Fort Courage
63. The wisecracking extraterrestrial's name was an acronym for Alien Life Form.
64. Bob woke up and was back in the bedroom of his character Bob Hartley, from *The Bob Newhart Show* with wife Emily (Suzanne Pleshette).
65. U.S. Grant
66. Sweat-hogs
67. A red Thunderbird
68. Laura Palmer
69. Audrey Meadows

70. Mel Tormé
71. Black Beauty
72. Bunny
73. A veterinarian played by Burgess Meredith (*Batman*'s Penguin)
74. They were sisters.
75. Auto racing
76. In his shoe
77. Geraldine Jones
78. Hoss, played by Dan Blocker
79. *The Los Angeles Sun*
80. His Uncle Martin
81. *That Girl.* Ted Bessell played Donald, and Lew Parker played Lou.
82. *The Ghost and Mrs. Muir* starred Hope Lange and Edward Mulhare as Carolyn Muir and Captain Daniel Gregg. Ms. Lange won two Emmys for her work on the show.
83. She was a ghost.
84. Jaleel White played Steve Urkel on *Family Matters*.
85. *Tool Time*
86. Jose Feliciano
87. Rising star Freddie Prinze, who played Chico, committed suicide in 1977.
88. Cosmo; a coffee table-shaped book about coffee tables
89. Robert Wagner; Fred Astaire
90. He married his maid so she wouldn't be deported.
91. Hutch, played by David Soul
92. Lucy loved *Three's Company*.
93. Angel and Spike
94. *Alice Doesn't Live Here Anymore;* Vic Tayback played Mel, the diner owner, in both the film and the series. Diane Ladd played Flo in the film and Belle, a waitress who took Flo's place in the series when the character (played on TV by Polly Holliday) was spun-off into *Flo*.
95. "Kiss my grits!"
96. Roseanne's husband, Dan
97. *The Invisible Man*
98. John Lacey, played by Judd Hirsch
99. An explosion caused the moon to be dislodged from its orbit of Earth.
100. Ann Sothern
101. Tom Wopat played Jeff
102. She revealed that she was gay.

103. Jerry Robinson, the dentist
104. A solar-powered hovercraft; Rem
105. Roddy McDowall played Galen in the TV series, and two characters in the films: Cornelius and Caesar.
106. Salty
107. Leonard Nimoy
108. World War II
109. Aliens abducted his younger sister.
110. *Diff'rent Strokes*
111. Tim Daly locked horns with the one-armed man.
112. Tennis
113. Alzheimer's
114. Kaye Ballard and Eve Arden
115. Frank Oz

Golden Oldies
116. Gale Storm; New York City
117. Betty White; insurance salesman
118. *I Married Joan*; Joan and Bradley Stevens
119. *Pete and Gladys* (Cara Williams played Gladys, a character mentioned but not seen on *December Bride*.)
120. They played film stars in *Mr. Adams and Eve*.
121. Joan Caulfield played Liz from 1953 to '55; Vanessa Brown took over the role in 1955. Liz's husband, George (Barry Nelson) was a banker.
122. Ricky Nelson
123. German shepherd; Rusty
124. Ruth Warrick
125. Barbara Eden played nearsighted Loco.
126. Red Connors

Game Shows
127. Tinkle
128. "Come on down!"
129. *Win, Lose or Draw.* The set was even designed to resemble Burt's living room.
130. Dick Clark
131. Vanna White wasn't the first person to perform the job, but she's made a career of it.

132. They pulled a big handle like those on slot machines.
133. Dr. Joyce Brothers
134. Regis Philbin; Meredith Vieira
135. *The Weakest Link*
136. A fake duck descended, holding prize money.
137. Whoopi Goldberg

Short-Lived Shows

138. She had ESP. The newlyweds were played by Sally Field and John Davidson.
139. Jennifer Aniston
140. Jodie Foster
141. At Kellerman's, a resort in the Catskills; Patrick Cassidy
142. *People*
143. *Hail to the Chief*; Ted Bessell
144. *Bob Patterson*
145. The Ansonia; *Big Shamus, Little Shamus*
146. *That 80s Show*
147. *Life with Lucy*
148. She was a staff psychiatrist at a police department.
149. Chevy Chase's *The Chevy Chase Show*, ran from September 7 to October 15, 1993—several weeks too long, in the opinion of most critics.

Costumed Superheroes

150. Harriet Cooper (Madge Blake) was Bruce's dowdy aunt.
151. Eartha Kitt, Lee Meriwether, and Julie Newmar
152. Two: Wednesdays and Thursdays
153. Central City; John Wesley Shipp
154. The Hall of Justice; Ted Knight
155. It was invisible.
156. She deflected bullets with them.
157. *Playgirl*
158. Debra Winger
159. Billy Batson
160. She pulled out her magic necklace and exclaimed, "O mighty Isis!"
161. Elvis Presley
162. Green
163. Lara Parker, who also played Angelique on *Dark Shadows*

164. Elvis played twins in *Kissin' Cousins* (1964). Yvonne played Azalea Tatum the girlfriend of one of the brothers.

165. Thermoman

166. He was bitten by a radioactive spider.

167. *The Greatest American Hero*, starring William Katt

168. *Captain Nice*

169. Deidre Hall has played Marlena Evans Brady on and off since 1976.

The 1990s and Beyond

170. Central Perk

171. Zoe

172. She bought a car, then died in an auto accident.

173. *Home Alone*'s Macaulay Culkin

174. Just Jack!

175. Old, unsolved cases

176. *American Idol*

177. Judge Advocate General

178. They're dubbed The Fab Five.

179. Lucille Ball

180. A cat and a mouse

181. Blair Brown

182. *Enterprise*

183. *The Real World*

184. Special Victims Unit

185. Jayne Mansfield, who died in an auto accident when Mariska was a child (Mariska was in the back seat with two of Jayne's other children, and all three survived.)

186. Café Nervosa

187. She was hired to be the live-in physical therapist for Fraiser and Niles' dad, Martin.

188. She had one disco hit.

189. John Ritter

190. Lennie Briscoe (Jerry Orbach)

191. Richard Hatch

192. David Caruso, in a shower scene

193. Kim Delaney

194. She went into the witness relocation program.

195. *Fear Factor*

196. Sheindlin
197. A crashing helicopter fell on him outside the entrance to the emergency room.
198. Sharon Stone
199. Kyle
200. Paris Hilton and Nicole Richie

PART II
Classic Quizzes

The Munsters
Moonlighting
Mork & Mindy
The Odd Couple
The Patty Duke Show
Petticoat Junction
Saturday Night Live
The Simpsons
Star Trek
Taxi
Three's Company

The Addams Family

1964–66, starring John Astin, Carolyn Jones, Jackie Coogan

1. What did Gomez like to do with his toy trains?
2. What language would Morticia speak in, to turn Gomez on?
3. What was Morticia's maiden name?
4. What was Morticia's artistic hobby?
5. What was the name of Morticia's carnivorous plant?
6. Name the two Addams children.
7. What was unusual about the daughter's doll, Marie Antoinette?
8. Who played Morticia's wacky sister? What was the character's name?
9. What famous movie witch played Morticia's mother, Esther?
10. Describe Cousin Itt.
11. Describe Thing.
12. In the episode "Morticia's Romance," Gomez and Morticia were celebrating their wedding anniversary. How long had they been married?
13. The actress who guest-starred as Lurch's mother played the grandmother of a very different family, *The Waltons*. Name her.
14. All but one of the primary cast members reunited for the TV movie *Halloween with the Addams Family* in 1977. Who wasn't there?
15. What prolific TV producer was Carolyn Jones married to from 1953 to '65?
16. Carolyn Jones had an amusing cameo in one of Marilyn Monroe's biggest hit movies. Which one?

The Addams Family—Answers

1. Crash them
2. French
3. Frump
4. Painting
5. Cleopatra
6. Pugsley and Wednesday
7. She was headless.
8. Carolyn Jones pulled double duty, portraying Morticia as well as her sister, Ophelia Frump.
9. Esther was played by Margaret Hamilton, most famous for portraying the Wicked Witch of the West in the film classic *The Wizard of Oz*.
10. He was covered with hair, from head to foot.
11. It was a very mobile disembodied hand, in a box.
12. Thirteen years
13. Ellen Corby played Mother Lurch in the 1965 episode "Mother Lurch Visits the Addams Family."
14. Blossom Rock, who played Grandmama
15. Aaron Spelling
16. In *The Seven Year Itch*, Carolyn played Miss Finch, an amorous night nurse who tries to convince a patient to steal an ambulance and run away with her (in his daydream).

Adventures of Superman

1953–57, starring George Reeves, Phyllis Coates, Noel Neill, Jack Larson, John Hamilton

1. Name Superman's biological parents, who, in the first episode, put him in a rocket and blasted him into space before his home world of Krypton exploded. What was Superman's Kryptonian name?
2. On the show, Superman's adoptive parents had different names than they had in the comic book series. What were their TV names?
3. What was the name of the town where Superman grew up, in the guise of mild-mannered Clark Kent?
4. What material did Superman's adoptive mother use to create his super uniform?
5. Name the newspaper where Clark Kent and company worked, and the city where it was located.
6. Name the plucky girl reporter who never figured out that her coworker Clark Kent and Superman were the same person.
7. Did Perry White, the boss of the newsroom, insist on being called Chief?
8. What phrase would Perry cry out when surprised or annoyed?
9. Name the absent-minded professor who stirred up trouble for Superman several episodes including "All That Glitters" (the final show of the series).
10. Fill in the blank: In the opening credits Superman was described as a "_____ visitor from another planet…"
11. What kind of stone could cause harm to Superman?
12. At the beginning of the show's second season, in 1953, there was a major cast change. Which character was recast?
13. The episode "Flight to the North" featured a character whose last name was Superman. What future star of a TV western played him?
14. Which *Adventures of Superman* cast member had a role in the 1939 blockbuster film *Gone With the Wind*?
15. Which cast member took his own life in 1959?
16. What part did Noel Neill play in the 1978 film *Superman: The Movie*?

Adventures of Superman—Answers

1. Jor-El and Lara were the parents of Kal-El.
2. Eben and Sarah Kent. (In the comics, and in other TV incarnations, they were Jonathan and Martha Kent.)
3. Smallville
4. The baby blankets he was wrapped in when he arrived on Earth
5. *The Daily Planet* in Metropolis
6. Lois Lane
7. No. In fact, when cub reporter Jimmy Olsen called him that, he'd angrily exclaim, "Don't call me Chief!"
8. "Great Cesar's Ghost!"
9. Professor Pepperwinkle
10. Strange
11. Kryptonite
12. Lois Lane; Noel Neill took over from Phyllis Coates.
13. Chuck Connors, later star of the *Rifleman*
14. George Reeves played Stuart Tarleton, one of Scarlett O'Hara's many suitors.
15. George Reeves
16. She had a very brief, uncredited cameo as Lois Lane's mother.

All in the Family

**1971–79, starring Caroll O'Connor, Jean Stapleton,
Sally Struthers, Rob Reiner
Name changed to *Archie Bunker's Place*, 1979–83**

1. What New York City borough was the setting of *All in the Family*?
2. Who sang the show's theme song, "Those Were the Days"?
3. Where was Archie Bunker stationed during World War II?
4. What medal did Archie earn during the war?
5. What were Archie's two jobs for the first several seasons?
6. What did Archie do for a living after he was laid off from his primary job?
7. What was Edith's job?
8. What brand of beer did Archie drink?
9. Which Rat Pack member visited the Bunker home and got the honor of sitting in Archie's chair?
10. What was Archie's nickname for his son-in-law, Mike Stivic?
11. What was Archie's nickname for his wife, Edith?
12. What was the name of Archie and Edith's grandson?
13. What was Edith's maiden name?
14. What was Edith's favorite soap opera?
15. Which character, who would later be spun-off into his own series, was introduced in the 1973 episode "Henry's Farewell"?
16. After Mike and Gloria moved to California and left the show, a little girl named Stephanie came to live with Archie and Edith. How was Stephanie related to them?
17. Which main character died of a stroke when *All in the Family* became *Archie Bunker's Place*?
18. In the *Archie Bunker's Place* episode "Gloria Comes Home," Sally Struthers returned as Archie's daughter, then was spun-off into her own series. Name the spin-off.
19. Who played Veronica Rooney, the cook, on *Archie Bunker's Place*?
20. What museum now houses Archie's chair?

21. What was the Bunkers' street address?

22. A very-short lived 1994 Norman Lear sitcom was set in the same house the Bunkers had lived in. This time a black family, headed by a character played by John Amos, lived there. What was the name of this show?

All in the Family—**Answers**

1. Queens
2. Carroll O'Connor and Jean Stapleton, in character as Archie and Edith Bunker
3. He was stationed first in Fort Riley, Kansas, and later in Italy.
4. A Purple Heart
5. He was a dock foreman at a tool and die company, and he drove a cab to earn extra money.
6. He bought his favorite hangout, Kelsey's Bar, and renamed it Archie Bunker's Place.
7. She was a Sunshine Lady at the Sunshine Home for the Elderly.
8. Schlitz
9. Sammy Davis Jr.
10. Meathead
11. Dingbat
12. Joey Stivic (A doll based on Joey was the first anatomically correct baby male doll.)
13. Baines
14. *As the World Turns*
15. George Jefferson, played by Sherman Hemsley
16. Edith
17. Stephanie (played by Danielle Brisebois) was Edith's niece
18. *Gloria*
19. Anne Meara
20. The Smithsonian
21. 704 Houser
22. *704 Houser*

The Andy Griffith Show

1960–68, starring Andy Griffith, Don Knotts, Frances Bavier

1. Andy Taylor was introduced on another sitcom, then spun-off into *The Andy Griffith Show*. What show spawned Andy?
2. During the first season, Andy dated a lady druggist. Name the character and the actress who played her.
3. What was the last name of Andy's bumbling deputy, Barney?
4. What was the name of Goober Pyle's cousin, who was spun-off into his own series when he joined the Marines? Name the actor who played him.
5. How did Helen Crump first encounter the Taylor family?
6. Andy and Helen finally got married in the first episode of an *Andy Griffith Show* spin-off. Name the spin-off and its star.
7. What was Floyd Lawson's occupation?
8. In his small town of Mayberry, North Carolina, did Andy have a patrol car?
9. What future film director played freckle-faced kid Opie Taylor?
10. What was the name of the hillbilly family that sometimes crossed paths with Andy?
11. What was Andy's full name?
12. Did Andy and/or Barney carry guns?
13. What street did the Taylors live on?
14. What type of musical instrument did Andy enjoy playing on his front porch?
15. When Barney left Mayberry to take a job at the Raleigh Police Department, who replaced him as deputy?
16. Raleigh was one of Mayberry's neighboring towns. What was the other nearby town that was often mentioned?
17. What was Aunt Bee's catchphrase?
18. What was the name of Barney's best girl?
19. What was the name of the gas station where Goober worked?
20. What crime did Otis Campbell repeatedly commit?
21. Which one of *The Beverly Hillbillies* guest-starred in the episode "Opie's Hobo Friend" as Opie's hobo friend?

22. Which *Gilligan's Island* castaway played a farmer who pursed Barney's girl-friend in the episode "The Farmer Takes a Wife"?

23. On several 1965 episodes, the Taylors were in Hollywood while a movie based on Andy's life was being shot. What was the name of the movie?

24. Who was the driving teacher in the episode "Aunt Bee Learns to Drive"?

25. What future star of such films as *Chinatown* and *As Good As It Gets* guest-starred as a man on trial in "Aunt Bee, Juror"?

26. In the high-rated 1986 TV reunion movie *Return to Mayberry*, Opie had grown up and married. What was his job?

The Andy Griffith Show—Answers

1. Audiences first saw Andy on *The Danny Thomas Show* in February 1960.
2. Ellie Walker, played by Elinor Donahue, worked at Walker Drug Store, owned by her father, Fred Walker.
3. Fife
4. Gomer Pyle, played by Jim Nabors
5. As Opie's schoolteacher
6. *Mayberry RFD*; Ken Berry
7. Barber
8. Yes
9. Ron Howard
10. The Darlings
11. Andrew Jackson Taylor
12. Andy did not carry a gun. Barney did, but Andy only allowed him to carry one bullet.
13. Maple
14. Guitar
15. Deputy Warren Ferguson, played by Jack Burns
16. Mount Pilot
17. "Oh, fiddle-faddle!"
18. Thelma Lou, played by Betty Lynn
19. Wally's Filling Station
20. Otis was the town drunk. He locked himself in Andy's jail when he got intoxicated, then let himself out when he sobered up.
21. Buddy Ebsen (Jed Clampett)
22. Alan Hale Jr. (The Skipper)
23. *Sheriff Without a Gun*
24. Goober
25. Jack Nicholson
26. He was editor of the local newspaper, *The Mayberry Gazette*.

Batman

1966–68, starring Adam West, Burt Ward, Yvonne Craig

Guest-starring on *Batman* as a wacky villain became a status symbol—some of the biggest stars of the day donned colorful costumes and spouted silly dialogue. Match the villains with the stars who played them:

1. The Archer	**A.** David Wayne
2. Black Widow	**B.** Shelley Winters
3. The Bookworm	**C.** Carolyn Jones
4. Chandell	**D.** Art Carney
5. Clock King	**E.** Maurice Evans
6. Dr. Cassandra	**F.** Frank Gorshin and John Astin
7. Egghead	**G.** Victor Buono
8. King Tut	**H.** Cliff Robertson
9. Louie The Lilac	**I.** Milton Berle
10. Lord Fogg	**J.** Joan Collins
11. Ma Parker	**K.** Zsa Zsa Gabor
12. Marsha, Queen Of Diamonds	**L.** Liberace
13. The Mad Hatter	**M.** Van Johnson
14. The Minstrel	**N.** George Sanders, Otto Preminger, and Eli Wallach
15. Minerva	**O.** Tallulah Bankhead
16. Mr. Freeze	**P.** Walter Slezak
17. The Puzzler	**Q.** Ida Lupino
18. The Riddler	**R.** Roddy McDowall
19. Shame	**S.** Vincent Price
20. The Siren	**T.** Rudy Vallee

Batman—Answers

1. The Archer…**D.** Art Carney
2. Black Widow…**O.** Tallulah Bankhead
3. The Bookworm…**R.** Roddy McDowall
4. Chandell…**L.** Liberace
5. Clock King…**P.** Walter Slezak
6. Dr Cassandra…**Q.** Ida Lupino
7. Egghead…**S.** Vincent Price
8. King Tut…**G.** Victor Buono
9. Louie The Lilac…**I.** Milton Berle
10. Lord Fogg…**T.** Rudy Vallee
11. Ma Parker…**B.** Shelley Winters
12. Marsha, Queen Of Diamonds…**C.** Carolyn Jones
13. The Mad Hatter…**A.** David Wayne
14. The Minstrel…**M.** Van Johnson
15. Minerva…**K.** Zsa Zsa Gabor
16. Mr. Freeze…**N.** George Sanders, Otto Preminger, and Eli Wallach
17. The Puzzler…**E.** Maurice Evans
18. The Riddler…**F.** Frank Gorshin and John Astin
19. Shame…**H.** Cliff Robertson
20. The Siren…**J.** Joan Collins

The Beverly Hillbillies

1962–71, starring Buddy Ebsen, Irene Ryan, Donna Douglas, Max Baer Jr., Nancy Kulp, Raymond Bailey

1. How did the Clampetts strike it rich?
2. Which family member was particularly fond of "critters"?
3. What was the name of Mr. Drysdale's plucky secretary? Who played her? Which other character did she carry the torch for?
4. Who were the Clampetts' next-door neighbors?
5. What did the hillbillies call their swimming pool?
6. In a curly blonde wig and a frilly dress, what female role did macho Max Baer Jr. (Jethro) play during the show's first season?
7. What type of wildlife did Miss Jane enjoy observing?
8. Name the country music musicians who performed the theme song ("The Ballad of Jed Clampett") and occasionally guest-starred on the show.
9. What movie spy did Jethro often emulate?
10. What country singer played Cousin Roy in the episode "Cousin Roy in Movieland"?
11. What kind of animal was the Clampetts' pet, Duke?
12. What was Granny's real name, and how was she related to Jed?
13. What type of beverage did Granny brew by the pool?
14. What was the name of the oil company that made old Jed a millionaire?
16. What was the name of Mr. Drysdale's bank, where Jed's millions were kept?
17. Who originally owned the truck that carried the Clampetts to Beverly Hills?
18. What was the name of the big Hollywood movie studio that Jed bought?
19. What catchphrase did Jed often exclaim?
20. How far did Jethro make it in school?
21. What was the town "back home," where the Clampetts went to see movies at the Bijou?
22. What former silent movie queen was one of their favorite actresses, whom they met in Beverly Hills and made a movie with?
23. In the 1969 episode "Jed Inherits a Castle," where was the castle?

24. What was the name of the dashing actor who fell in love with Elly May?

25. Who played Granny's ma in the 1981 reunion TV movie, *The Return of the Beverly Hillbillies?*

The Beverly Hillbillies—**Answers**

1. Jed (Buddy Ebsen) struck oil on his property while hunting.
2. Elly May
3. Miss Jane Hathaway was played by Nancy Kulp. She carried a torch for handsome but naive Jethro.
4. The Drysdales
5. "The cement pond"
6. Jethro's sister, Jethrine Bodine
7. Birds
8. Lester Flatt and Earl Scurggs
9. Bond. James Bond
10. Roy Clark
11. A bloodhound
12. Daisy Moses was Jed's mother-in-law, making her Elly May's "Granny."
13. She made moonshine.
14. O.K. Oil Company, based in Tulsa, Oklahoma.
16. Commerce Bank of Beverley Hills
17. Pearl, Jethro's ma, owned the truck, a 1920 Oldsmobile.
18. Mammoth Film Studios
19. "Well, Doggies!"
20. He graduated the 6th grade.
21. Bugtussle
22. Gloria Swanson. The movie (a silent) was called *Passion's Plaything*.
23. London
24. Dash Riprock
25. Irene Ryan had died, so Imogene Coca filled the "perky senior citizen" type role.

Bewitched

1964–72, starring Elizabeth Montgomery, Agnes Moorehead, Dick York, Dick Sargent

1. What major confession did Samantha make to Darrin on the very first episode, "I, Darrin, Take This Witch, Samantha"?

2. What was Darrin's nickname for Samantha?

3. How did Samantha summon the witches' physician, Doctor Bombay?

4. What did Aunt Clara collect?

5. Name Darrin and Samantha's two children.

6. Which *Bewitched* character was spun-off into her own 1977–78 series?

7. Elizabeth Montgomery made her TV debut on her movie star dad's 1950–57 anthology series. Name the series.

8. Who played Samantha's dark-haired, bad-girl cousin, Serena?

9. What did the names of nearly all the female witches on *Bewitched* have in common?

10. What color was Endora's hair?

11. Which famous magical creature did Imogene Coca guest star as?

12. At the beginning of the fourth season, Samantha was bestowed with a special witchy honor. What happened?

13. For the first several seasons, Samantha wore a distinctive pendant on a chain in nearly every episode. What shape was the pendant?

14. What street did the Stephenses live on?

15. When upset by the magical happenings in his home, where did Darrin go to drown his sorrows?

16. Name Samantha's father and the actor who played him.

17. In a 1964 episode, Samantha introduced a crabby orphan boy (played by Billy Mumy of *Lost in Space*) to a magical man. Who was the man and where did he live?

18. Nancy Kovack guest-starred in several episodes (including the first) as Darrin's ex-girlfriend. What was her character's name?

19. What happened to Esmeralda whenever she got upset?

20. What body part did Samantha twitch to practice magic?

21. What future star of *The Jeffersons* guest-starred as a housekeeper in the episode "Samantha Goes South for a Spell"?

22. What primetime cartoon did Samantha and Darrin guest-star on?

23. Name the two actresses who played Louise Tate.

24. What game show did Paul Lynde (Uncle Arthur) star in, occupying the center square?

25. Which cast member played Peter Parker's overbearing boss in the 1977 TV movie *The Amazing Spiderman*?

Bewitched—Answers

1. She told him she was a witch.
2. Sam
3. If she yelled "Calling, Dr. Bombay! Calling Dr. Bombay!" he would appear in her home.
4. Doorknobs
5. Tabitha and Adam
6. Samantha's magical daughter was the title character of *Tabitha*. Lisa Hartman starred.
7. *Robert Montgomery Presents*
8. Elizabeth Montgomery donned a black wig to play the part. In some episodes credit went to a made-up actress: Pandora Spocks.
9. They ended in the letter "a." (Endora, Samantha, Esmeralda, Clara, et al.)
10. Red
11. She played Mary, the Good Fairy (the tooth fairy), who tricked Samantha into taking over her tooth-gathering duties.
12. She was crowned Queen of the Witches, much to Darrin's dismay.
13. It was a heart-shaped pendant from Elizabeth Montgomery's personal jewelry collection (a gift from her husband, *Bewitched* producer Bill Asher).
14. Morning Glory Circle
15. Joe's Bar and Grill
16. Maurice was played by Maurice Evans.
17. Samantha took him to the North Pole to meet Santa Claus in the episode "A Vision of Sugar Plums."
18. Sheila
19. She gradually disappeared.
20. Her nose
21. Isabelle Sanford
22. *The Flintstones*
23. Irene Vernon and Kasey Rogers
24. *Hollywood Squares*
25. David White, who played Darrin's overbearing boss, Larry Tate

The Brady Bunch

1969–74, starring Florence Henderson, Robert Reed, Ann B. Davis

1. What was the name of the kids' two pets, seen in the first few episodes, and what kind of animals were they?
2. Name all six Brady kids.
3. What was the name of the kids' young cousin, who joined the family near the series' end—and who played him?
4. What was Mike Brady's occupation?
5. What was the name of the singing group the kids formed?
6. How did Cindy and Bobby attempt to set a world record in their backyard?
7. Who guest-starred as the less-than-gorgeous title character in the episode "Jan's Aunt Jenny"?
8. What type of idol did Bobby discover during the family's Hawaiian vacation?
9. What classic horror movie star guest-starred during the Hawaiian episodes? What character did he play?
10. What pop music star did Marcia invite to sing at her high school prom?
11. In the final episode, "The Hair-Brained Scheme," Bobby accidentally dyed Greg's hair an unusual color, just before Greg's high school graduation ceremony. What color?
12. What star of *Dark Shadows* and the film *Willy Wonka and the Chocolate Factory* guest-starred as Peter's blind date in the episode "Two Petes in a Pod"?
13. What is the occupation of Alice's boyfriend, Sam?
14. Name Alice's look-alike cousin who substituted for Alice while she took a much-needed vacation.
15. What was the name of Cindy's doll?
16. Name Jan and Marcia's grooms, whom they married on the 1981 spin-off *The Brady Brides*.
17. Which Brady girl developed a drinking problem on the 1990 dramatic spin-off *The Bradys*?
18. Which former MTV veejay played Bobby's wife, Tracy, on *The Bradys*?
19. Which cast member opted not to take part in *The Brady Bunch Hour*?

20. Which cast member opted not to take part in *The Bradys*?

21. What was the name of the 1972–74 Saturday morning animated series featuring the Brady kids?

22. What Emmy-winning *Cheers* star played Carol in the 1995 big-screen hit *The Brady Bunch Movie*?

23. What future *Little House on the Prairie* star played the girl who gave Peter his first kiss?

24. Was Mike Brady's first wife (the boys' mother) ever seen on the show?

25. What did Carol start doing for a living after the kids grew up?

26. What street did the Bradys live on?

27. What Girl Scout-like group did Marcia belong to?

28. What was the name of the ice cream parlor where Jan and Marcia briefly worked?

29. In the 1970 episode "The Not-So-Ugly Duckling," Jan pretended to have a boyfriend. What was his see-through name?

The Brady Bunch—**Answers**

1. A cat named Fluffy and a dog named Tiger. Tiger's doghouse remained in the backyard for years, but early in the first season both animals were gone, without any explanation.
2. Marcia, Greg, Jan, Peter, Cindy, and Bobby
3. Oliver was played by Robbie Rist.
4. He was an architect, which was ironic since the Brady home had a few architectural defects, including one bathroom shared by six kids.
5. The Brady Six
6. Teeter-tottering
7. Imogene Coca
8. A cursed tiki doll
9. Vincent Price played Professor Whitehead. (He also later guest-starred on *The Brady Bunch Hour*.)
10. Davy Jones
11. Orange
12. Denise Nickerson
13. Butcher (He owned Sam's Butcher Shop.)
14. Emma, who, of course, was also played by Ann B. Davis
15. Kitty Carry-All
16. Wally Logan (Marcia's hubby) and Phillip Covington III (Jan's)
17. Marcia
18. Martha Quinn
19. Eve Plumb
20. Maureen McCormick
21. *The Brady Kids*
22. Shelley Long
23. Melissa Sue Anderson
24. The dead character's photo was very briefly shown on the first episode.
25. She became a real estate agent.
26. Clinton Avenue
27. She was a Sunflower Girl.
28. Hanson's Ice Cream Parlor
29. George Glass

Cheers

1982–93, starring Ted Danson, Shelley Long, Kirstie Alley

1. What real Boston watering hole was the bar Cheers based on?
2. What Tony-winning actress played Sam's date, Debra, in the series' second episode, "Sam's Women"?
3. What was Diane's job before she came to work at Cheers?
4. What was Sam's nickname when he played for the Boston Red Sox?
5. Which future star of *Moonlighting* guest-starred as Coach's daughter, Lisa?
6. In the episode "Truth or Consequences," Carla tested Diane's ability to keep a secret by telling her a lie. What was the lie?
7. Runaway bride Diane left two *Cheers* characters at the altar—which ones?
8. In the episode "Endless Slumper," Sam loaned a friend his lucky bottle cap. What was the significance of the cap?
9. Actress Glynis Johns played Diane's mother in the episode "Someone Single, Someone Blue." Glynis also played a mom in a classic 1964 Disney movie about a magical nanny. Name the film.
10. What was the name of Norm's wife, who was often talked about but never clearly seen on the show?
11. What did Fraiser's mother, Hester, threaten to do if Diane kept dating her son, in the episode "Diane Meets Mom"?
12. Which Cheers regular was a mailman who lived with his mother?
13. On one of the few episodes to venture outside the bar, where did the gang have dinner in "Thanksgiving Orphans"?
14. Which Monty Python regular guest-starred as a marriage counselor trying to help Sam and Diane in the episode "Simon Says"?
15. Why did Diane leave Cheers (and Sam) in the episode "I Do, Adieu"?
16. Before finding success as an actress, what game show did Kirstie Alley (Rebecca) appear on?
17. What was the name of Lilith and Fraiser's son?
18. What multiple Tony-winner (for *Torch Song Trilogy, La Cage aux Folles,* and *Hairspray*) played Rebecca's gay former flame on "Rebecca's Lover...Not"?

19. How did the bar patrons respond every time Norm entered the bar?
20. How did the final episode of *Cheers* end?
21. Which character was spun-off at the end of *Cheers'* run?

Cheers—Answers

1. The Bull & Finch
2. Donna McKechnie, who won a Tony for her work in *A Chorus Line*
3. Diane was the teaching assistant of Professor Sumner Sloane—and she was having an affair with him.
4. Mayday Malone
5. Allyce Beasley
6. She told Diane that Sam was the father of one of her many children.
7. Sam Malone and Fraiser Crane
8. It was the bottle cap from the last beer alcoholic Sam drank.
9. *Mary Poppins*
10. Vera
11. She threatened to kill Diane. Nancy Marchand, who played Hester, went on to play another murderous mom on *The Sopranos*.
12. Cliff Clavin
13. At Carla's house
14. John Cleese won an Emmy for this guest spot.
15. Because Shelley Long was leaving the series, Diane left town to finish writing a book.
16. *Match Game*
17. Frederick Crane
18. They called out his name.
19 Harvey Fierstein was nominated for an Emmy for this performance.
20. Sam closed up the bar for the night and walked into the back room.
21. Diane's ex, Fraiser Crane, moved to Seattle to become the host of a radio talk show and the main character of *Fraiser*.

Dallas

1978–91, starring Larry Hagman, Barbara Bel Geddes, Patrick Duffy

1. What underwater sci-fi series starred Patrick Duffy before he played Bobby Ewing?
2. In the media-hyped storyline, "Who shot J.R.?"
3. Which cast member was once married to rock star Elvis Presley? What part did she play?
4. What short-lived sci-fi show, set in the Bermuda Triangle, starred Jared Martin (Sue Ellen's boyfriend Dusty) as a telepath named Varian?
5. How was Bobby's return explained when the dead character showed up, very much alive, in Pam's shower?
6. After her beloved Jock died, whom did Miss Ellie marry?
7. Name the Ewing family's Texas ranch, where much of *Dallas* took place.
8. What former classic sitcom star briefly took over the role of Miss Ellie?
9. Who played Adam, a devilish character tormenting J.R., in the final episode?
10. What did the initials J.R. stand for?
11. What was the source of the Ewing family fortune?
12. How were Pam and Cliff related?
13. In the show's 14th season, in 1990, a daytime soap diva briefly joined the cast as Sheila Foley for a story arc in which Sheila killed Bobby's wife, April, in Paris. Who was the Daytime-Emmy-winning diva?
14. In 1981, another big Daytime-Emmy-winner, Susan Flannery, briefly played Leslie Stewart, one of J.R.'s business associates. What was her specialty?
15. A co-star from Larry Hagman's sitcom past guest-starred in 1991 as Lee Ann Nelson De La Vega, a former flame bent on J.R.'s destruction. Who was the guest-star?
16. What were the names of Lucy's parents, who were spun-off into *Knots Landing*?
17. Who was the biological mother of Christopher, the child adopted by Bobby and Pam?

18. Which star of *Dark Shadows* was a former Playboy Bunny who played a character named Bunny in a few 1989 episodes?

19. Which cast member originated the part of Maggie in *Cat on a Hot Tin Roof* on Broadway?

20. Which character turned out to be Jock's illegitimate son?

Dallas—**Answers**

1. Duffy played *The Man From Atlantis*.
2. His sister-in-law, Kristin
3. Priscilla Presley played Jenna Wade, Bobby's childhood sweetheart.
4. *Fantastic Journey*
5. Pam had dreamed the entire previous season, including Bobby's death and elaborate funeral.
6. Clayton Farlow, played by Howard Keel
7. Southfork
8. Donna Reed
9. *Cabaret* star Joel Grey
10. John Ross
11. Oil
12. They were brother and sister.
13. Susan Lucci (Erica on *All My Children*)
14. She was a public relations expert.
15. Barbara Eden
16. Gary and Valene Ewing
17. Kristin, Sue Ellen's sister
18. Kathryn Leigh Scott
19. Barbara Bel Geddes
20. Ray Krebs

Dark Shadows

1966–71, starring Joan Bennett, Jonathan Frid, Louis Edmonds, Nancy Barrett, Lara Parker

1. What was the name of the spooky mansion where most of *Dark Shadows'* action took place?

2. What five words of narration started the very first episode?

3. The series started as a relatively traditional soap opera, then it took a serious supernatural turn when a monster played by Diana Millay showed up. Name Diana's character and the type of monster she was.

4. What was Victoria Winters' job at Collinwood? Who took over her duties when she literally vanished one day?

5. Why did Angelique curse Barnabas with vampirism?

6. Which one of *Charlie's Angels* made her TV debut on *DS* as a silent ghost? Name the quiet character.

7. What happened to Quentin Collins under the light of a full moon?

8. On what ABC soap opera did Louis Edmonds (Roger Collins) later play Langley Wallingford?

9. Name the two feature films based on *Dark Shadows*.

10. One of the characters played by Marie Wallace was inspired by the *Bride of Frankenstein*. Name the character and her intended mate.

11. What was the name of the present-time character played by Joan Bennett, a star from Hollywood's Golden Age? (Like other cast members, she played different characters in various time periods.)

12. What was distinctive about the walking stick carried by Barnabas Collins?

13. What future film star appeared in just one episode of *DS*, as a vampire named Audrey?

14. Name Collinsport's bar.

15. How were Carolyn and Elizabeth related?

16. Which Oliver Stone movie starred Jonathan Frid (Barnabas) after *DS* left the air? Which future *Fantasy Island* star was also in the film?

17. For what 1964 film did Grayson Hall (Julia Hoffman) receive an Academy Award nomination?

18. Who played Barnabas on the short-lived 1991 revival of *DS*, which aired in primetime?

19. What network did the original *DS* air on; what network presented the 1991 revival?

20. In the revival, Victoria (Joanna Going) was drawn into the past, where she met someone who looked exactly like her. Who was this look-alike?

21. In both versions of the show, Barnabas presented Josette with a distinctive gift—what was it?

Dark Shadows—**Answers**

1. Collinwood
2. "My name is Victoria Winters…"
3. Diana played Laura Collins, a phoenix.
4. She was governess to young David Collins; Maggie Evans took her job.
5. She loved him, but he didn't return her affection.
6. Kate Jackson played Daphne.
7. He turned into a werewolf.
8. *All My Children*
9. *House of Dark Shadows* and *Night of Dark Shadows*
10. Eve and Adam
11. Elizabeth Collins Stoddard
12. It featured a silver wolf's head.
13. Marsha Mason
14. The Blue Whale
15. Carolyn was Elizabeth's daughter.
16. Frid headed the cast of Stone's first film, *Seizure* (1974). Also in the cast: Herve' Villechaize, *Fantasy Island*'s Tattoo.
17. *Night of the Iguana*
18. Ben Cross (an ironic name for someone playing a vampire)
19. ABC; NBC
20. Josette
21. A music box

The Dick Van Dyke Show

1961–66, starring Dick Van Dyke, Mary Tyler Moore, Morey Amsterdam, Rose Marie

1. Rob, Sally, and Buddy were writers for what TV variety show?
2. What branch of the military was Rob in when he and Laura met and married? What town was he based in at the time?
3. What was Laura's maiden name?
4. What New York City suburb was home to Rob, Laura, and their son?
5. Name Rob and Laura's son—including his unusual middle name.
6. Who played Rob's boss, Alan Brady?
7. What type of clothing did Mary Tyler Moore wear as Laura, considered at first to be a bit risqué?
8. Who played Buddy?
9. Decades before she played Sally, Rose Marie was a child star, working in vaudeville. What was her stage name then?
10. What was the name of Buddy's wife, who was often mentioned on the show but never seen?
11. What recurring guest role did Dick Van Dyke's brother, Jerry Van Dyke, play?
12. What was the name of Laura's female neighbor and cohort?
13. What was the name of Alan Brady's male assistant?
14. What does the Petries' neighbor Jerry Helper do for a living?
15. What embarrassing fact about Alan Brady does Laura accidentally blurt out on a talk show in the episode "Coast-to-Coast Big Mouth"?
16. Suave Richard Dawson guest-starred in the episode "Racy Tracy Rattigan." Why was his character, Tracy, on the show?
17. Which star of *The Man from U.N.C.L.E.* played Laura's ex-boyfriend Jim Darling in the episode "It's a Shame She Married Me."
18. What popular 1964 Walt Disney musical did Dick Van Dyke star in, alongside Julie Andrews?

The Dick Van Dyke Show—**Answers**

1. *The Alan Brady Show*
2. The Army, based at Camp Crowder, in Joplin, Missouri
3. Laura Meeker
4. New Rochelle, New York
5. Ritchie Rosebud Petrie
6. Carl Reiner
7. Capri pants
8. Morey Amsterdam
9. Baby Rose Marie
10. Pickles
11. Rob's bashful brother, Stacey
12. Millie Helper
13. Melvin "Mel" Cooley, played by Richard Deacon
14. He was a dentist.
15. She revealed that Alan was bald and wore a toupee.
16. Tracy was guest-hosting *The Alan Brady Show* while Alan was out of town.
17. Robert Vaughn (Napoleon Solo on *U.N.C.L.E.*)
18. *Mary Poppins*

Dynasty

1981–89, starring John Forsythe, Linda Evans, Joan Collins

1. Name Blake Carrington's company.
2. What was the name of the Carringtons' butler?
3. Blake's ex-wife, Alexis, didn't show up until a season-ending-cliffhanger murder trial. Who was on trial, and for what?
4. Before she played spoiled-rotten Fallon Carrington Colby, what girl detective did Pamela Sue Martin play?
5. Before she took over the role of spoiled-rotten Fallon Carrington Colby, what soap opera detective did Emma Samms play?
6. When Steven Carrington was recast (Jack Coleman took over from Al Corley), how was the character's altered appearance explained?
7. When Emma Samms took over as Fallon, how was the change in Fallon's appearance explained?
8. Previously unmentioned Carrington children kept popping up as the series progressed. Name the son who'd been kidnapped as an infant, and the daughter Alexis was pregnant with when she left Denver years earlier.
9. Which Carrington daughter married a prince?
10. What African-American actress played Blake's singing half-sister?
11. Krystle's tennis pro ex-husband entered the scene in 1982 to stir things up. Name the character and the actor.
12. Name the two former movie greats who headed the cast of the *Dynasty* spin-off *The Colbys*.
13. The actress who played Constance Colby in *The Colbys* starred with Linda Evans (Krystle) in a 1965–69 TV western series; they played mother and daughter Victoria and Audra Barkley. Name the series.
14. Fallon had a fling with her doctor—a man who also tempted Krystle. Name this hard-to-resist physician and the actor who played him.
15. Joan Collins (Alexis)'s sister is the author of such mega-hit books as *Hollywood Wives* and *The Bitch*. Name her.

16. Alexis's sister wrote a tell-all novel about Alexis. Name the sister and the book.

17. Which cast member provided the voice of Charlie on *Charlie's Angels*?

18. Which cast member made a sappy 1970 movie in which her character told Ryan O'Neal's character, "Love means never having to say you're sorry."?

19. Which actor caused an uproar in Hollywood when it was announced he had AIDS—and he had kissed Linda Evans in a passionate *Dynasty* scene?

20. In the final episode of *The Colbys*, what unusual event happened to Fallon?

21. Which *Dynasty* star played a serial killer on the daytime soap *Days of Our Lives*?

Dynasty—**Answers**

1. The Denver-based Carrington company was called Denver-Carrington.

2. The butler, Joseph, was played by Lee Bergere.

3. Alexis arrived, in dark glasses and a big hat, to testify in the murder trial of Blake Carrington; he had killed his son's lover, Ted. (The glasses and hat concealed the fact that Alexis hadn't been cast yet; a stand-in played the part in that first appearance.)

4. Nancy Drew

5. Holly Scorpio on *General Hospital*

6. Steven had to have reconstructive plastic surgery after an accident.

7. It wasn't explained. Fallon's widower, Jeff Colby (John James), was shown talking to a painting of Fallon, in which she looked like Emma Samms, and in a later scene, Samms was seen as Fallon.

8. Adam was a kidnapping victim; Amanda was kept secret from her father, Blake.

9. Amanda, played by Catherine Oxenberg

10. Diahann Carroll portrayed Dominique Devereaux.

11. Geoffrey Scott played Mark Jennings, who had affairs with mother and daughter Alexis and Fallon.

12. *The Colbys* featured Charlton Heston as Jason Colby and Barbara Stanwyck as Jason's sister, Constance. Another actress primarily known for film work, Katherine Ross (*The Stepford Wives*), played Jeff's mother.

13. Barbara Stanwyck and Evans starred in *The Big Valley*. Lee Majors (*The Six Million Dollar Man*) was also in the cast.

14. Nick Toscanni was played by James Farentino.

15. Jackie Collins (Joan starred in the movie version of *The Bitch*.)

16. Caress penned *Sister Dearest*.

17. John Forsythe voiced the character, whose face was never shown.

18. Ali McGraw starred with O'Neal in *Love Story*. (In a later movie, the screwball comedy classic *What's Up, Doc?*, O'Neal poked fun at that line; when costar Barbara Streisand repeated it, he said it was the stupidest thing he'd ever heard.)

19. At the time it was revealed that Rock Hudson had AIDS, it was believed that the virus could be spread through kissing. Hudson briefly played Daniel Reece, a debonair horse-breeder on *Dynasty*.

20. She was abducted by a UFO.

21. Jack Coleman (Steven) played Jake, a handsome psycho, from 1981 to '82.

Friends

1994–2004, starring Courteney Cox, David Schwimmer, Jennifer Aniston, Lisa Kudrow, Matt LeBlanc, Matthew Perry

Which one of the friends…

1. …left her boyfriend at the altar in the first episode?
2. …was Monica's brother?
3. …was an actor with a starring role on the soap *Days of our Lives*?
4. …was played by the daughter of a real actor with a starring role on the soap *Days of our Lives*?
5. …had a father played by Kathleen Turner?
6. …had a twin sister named Ursula?
7. …had a pet monkey named Marcel?
8. …found a thumb in a can of soda?
9. …was a cleaning fanatic?
10. …was a really bad folk singer?
11. …dated Richard, played by former *Magnum, P.I.* detective Tom Selleck?
12. …dated the daughter of a character played by former *Moonlighting* detective Bruce Willis?
13. …had a haircut that became very popular in 1994?
14. …had a gay ex-wife?
15. …had a sexy romance novelist mother played by Morgan Fairchild?
16. …accidentally saw Rachel naked in the episode "The One With the Boobies"?
17. …married a Canadian ice dancer, so he could get a green card?
18. …had a mom played by *That Girl*'s Marlo Thomas?
19. …met Jean-Claude Van Damme on a movie set?
20. …perfected the pick-up line, "How you doin'?"?
21. …gave birth to triplets?
22. …married Monica?
23. …had Ross' daughter, Emma?
24. …employed a male nanny, played by Freddie Prinze Jr.?
25. …married Mike (Paul Rudd)?

Friends—**Answers**

1. Rachel
2. Ross
3. Joey
4. Rachel
5. Chandler
6. Phoebe
7. Ross
8. Phoebe
9. Monica
10. Phoebe (her signature song: "Smelly Cat")
11. Monica
12. Ross
13. Rachel
14. Ross
15. Chandler
16. Chandler
17. Phoebe
18. Rachel
19. Rachel and Monica
20. Joey
21. Phoebe
22. Chandler
23. Rachel
24. Rachel
25. Phoebe

Gilligan's Island

1964–67, starring Bob Denver, Alan Hale Jr., Jim Backus, Natalie Schafer, Tina Louise, Russell Johnson, Dawn Wells

1. What were the full names of the Skipper, the Professor, and Gilligan?
2. Which two characters were not named in the show's theme song for the first season?
3. In "The Hunter," a decidedly serious episode of the sitcom, Rory Calhoun guest starred as a big game hunter named Jonathan Kincaid. What did Kincaid do for sport on the island?
4. What child actor guest-starred as a jungle boy, then went on to become a grown-up movie star (and hunky husband of former *Laugh-In* star Goldie Hawn)?
5. How many seasons did *Gilligan's Island* last?
6. Were the castaways ever rescued?
7. What state was Mary Ann from?
8. What was Ginger's occupation?
9. Where did the group's doomed boat trip originate?
10. Jim Backus played Thurston Howell III. Was there a Thurston Howell IV?
11. In what Broadway play did Bob Denver (Gilligan) take over a role originated by Woody Allen?
12. On what popular nighttime soap did Tina Louise (Ginger) appear in 1978 and '79? What character did she play?
13. What was the name of the boat that brought the castaways to the island?
14. What glamorous blonde actress played a wealthy visitor to the island who was attracted to the Professor?
15. Bob Denver, Tina Louise, Russell Johnson, and Dawn Wells guest-starred on an episode of *Roseanne* in 1995. What was the premise of the episode?
16. Which cast member guest-starred on *I Dream of Jeannie* as a male genie?
17. Who was the creator of *Gilligan's Island*?
18. Bob Denver played a beatnik named Maynard G. Krebs on a classic 1959–63 sitcom. Name the show.

19. What was Mary Ann's last name?
20. What did the Skipper call Gilligan?
21. The Skipper and Gilligan slept in bunk-bed style hammocks. Who was on top?
22. What was the name of Mr. Howell's beloved teddy bear?
23. In the episode "Don't Bug the Mosquitoes," the women of the island formed a singing group. What was it called?
24. There were two Saturday morning cartoon series based on *Gilligan's Island*. Name both.
25. Did Mary Ann and Ginger share a hut, or did they each have their own?

Gilligan's Island—**Answers**

1. Jonas Grumby, Professor Roy Hinkley, and Willy Gilligan

2. At first the Professor and Mary Ann were referred to as "and the rest"; the lyrics were later changed to include them.

3. He hunted Gilligan like a wild animal.

4. Kurt Russell played a jungle boy who showed the castaways a helium outlet on the island. The Professor built a balloon that whisked the jungle boy off the island, but since he couldn't speak, the boy was unable to tell the sailors who rescued him about the castaways.

5. Three

6. Yes. The castaways were found in the 1978 TV movie, aptly titled *Rescue From Gilligan's Island*. The original cast members, with the exception of Tina Louise, reprised their roles. (Judith Baldwin filled Ginger's gown.)

7. Kansas

8. Actress ("movie star," according to the show's theme song)

9. Hawaii

10. Yes. Thurston IV showed up in the 1981 TV movie *The Harlem Globetrotters on Gilligan's Island*. He was played by David Ruprecht, later the host of the game show *Supermarket Sweep*.

11. Denver starred in *Play It Again, Sam*—and got good reviews.

12. Tina Louise played Julie Grey on *Dallas*.

13. The S.S. Minnow

14. Zsa Zsa Gabor played the title character in the episode "Erika Tiffany Smith to the Rescue." (Like other visitors to the island, she didn't actually rescue the castaways.)

15. Roseanne had a dream in which *Gilligan's Island* and *Roseanne* cast members swapped roles. For example, Bob Denver played Roseanne's sister Jackie, and Laurie Metcalf, who usually played Jackie, played Gilligan. On his official website (www.gilligan.com), Bob Denver said: "The biggest surprise for me when I walked into the *Roseanne* soundstage the first day of rehearsal was finding out that it was the same soundstage we used for *Gilligan's Island* over 30 years before."

16. Bob Denver

17. Sherwood Schwartz, who also created *The Brady Bunch*

18. *The Many Loves of Dobie Gillis*

19. Summers

20. Little Buddy

21. Gilligan

22. Teddy
23. The Honeybees
24. *The New Adventures of Gilligan* and *Gilligan's Planet*
25. They shared a hut.

Green Acres

1965–71, starring Eddie Albert, Eva Gabor

1. Who sold the rundown farm to Oliver? Who played the salesman?
2. Where did the Douglases live before moving to the country?
3. At first, how long does Lisa agree to stay at the farm?
4. What did Oliver have to do in order to make phone calls?
5. What was Oliver's occupation?
6. What was the name of the town nearest the Douglas farm?
7. Who ran the local general store?
8. What other rural sitcom, featuring the hotel The Shady Rest, had a lot of character crossovers with *Green Acres*?
9. What was the name of the Douglases' cow?
10. What country was Lisa from?
11. What college did Oliver attend?
12. Name the Douglases' farmhand and the actor who played him.
13. What did the farmhand call Oliver?
14. What radio show starring Bea Benaderet and Gale Gordon predated *Green Acres*, with the same basic plot, and a similar title?
15. What two Marilyn Monroe movies did Alvy Moore (Hank Kimball) have small roles in?
16. What did the Monroe siblings (Alf and Ralph) do for the Douglases?
17. What was the title of the *Green Acres* 1990 TV movie reunion?
18. In what two animated Disney movies did Eva Gabor and her fellow classic TV star Bob Newhart provide the voices of mice Bianca and Bernard?
19. What future *Hart to Hart* star was Eddie Albert's co-star in the 1975–79 detective series *Switch*?
20. In 1989 Eddie Albert guest-starred as the father of one of the main characters on *thirtysomething*. Which one?

Green Acres—**Answers**

1. Mr. Haney, played by Pat Buttram
2. New York City
3. Six months
4. He had to climb a phone pole.
5. Lawyer
6. Hooterville
7. Sam Drucker
8. *Petticoat Junction*
9. Eleanor
10. Hungary
11. Harvard Law School
12. Eb Dawson, played by Tom Lester
13. Dad
14. *Granby's Green Acres*, which aired from July 3 to August 21, 1950
15. They were carpenters, hired to expand the farmhouse. The lazy brother-sister team didn't get much carpentry done, though.
16. *Gentlemen Prefer Blondes* and *There's No Business Like Show Business*. Interestingly, he also appeared in *Move Over, Darling*, the 1963 Doris Day film which grew out of *Something's Got To Give*, the movie Marilyn was fired from shortly before her death. (It was retitled and Day took over the Monroe part.) In *Move Over, Darling*, Alvy played a room service waiter.
17. *Return to Green Acres*
18. *The Rescuers* (1977) and *The Rescuers Down Under* (1990)
19. Robert Wagner
20. He played Charlie Weston, the title character in the episode "Elliot's Dad." (Elliot was played by Timothy Busfield.)

Happy Days

1974–84, starring Marion Ross, Ron Howard, Henry Winkler

1. What type of store did Howard own?
2. Where did Fonzie live?
3. What was Fonzie's full name?
4. How old was Fonzie when his father deserted his family? What was his father's name?
5. What was Fonzie's nickname for Richie?
6. Was the Asian man who ran the kids' hangout, Arnold's, actually named Arnold?
7. Who took over Arnold's—and changed its name to his?
8. What was Fonzie's nickname for Joanie?
9. In a few early episodes, Richie and Joanie had an older brother. With no explanation, he was soon gone, never to be mentioned again. What was his name?
10. Name Joanie's boy-crazy best friend.
11. What extraterrestrial battled Fonzie before getting a show of his own?
12. Who was Fonzie's older dance partner in the episode "Dance Contest"?
13. How did Potsie get his nickname?
14. What was the name of the high school Richie attended?
15. When he met Lori Beth, whom he eventually married, what fraternity did Richie claim to be a member of?
16. The pilot for *Happy Days* was aired as part of another popular show. Name it.
17. On a two-parter titled "Fearless Fonzarelli," Fonzie performed a dangerous motorcycle stunt on a fictional reality show. Name that show.
18. In the 1975 episode that introduced the characters Laverne and Shirley, which two characters had blind dates with the girls?
19. What was the name of the Saturday morning cartoon show based on the show?
20. What motorcycle-riding, demolition-derby-competing tough chick did Fonzie almost marry on a three-part episode in 1976?

Happy Days—**Answers**

1. A hardware store called Cunningham Hardware
2. In an apartment over the Cunningham family's garage
3. Arthur Fonzerelli
4. Little Arthur was 3 years old when Vito left.
5. Red
6. No. The restaurant had that name when he took it over.
7. Al (Al Molinaro)
8. Shortcake
9. Chuck
10. Jenny Piccalo was mentioned but not shown for many years. In 1980, she entered the scene and became a main character.
11. Mork from Ork (Robin Williams) made his first appearance on a February 1978 episode of *Happy Days*, then got his own spin-off, *Mork & Mindy*.
12. Marion
13. His mom dubbed him Potsie because he made things out of clay.
14. Jefferson High School
15. Because he lived at home, he said he lived at "Mama Papa Sister."
16. *Love American Style*
17. *You Wanted to See It*
18. Richie and Fonzie
19. *The Fonz and the Happy Days Gang*. Cupcake, a girl from the future, was voiced by Didi Conn (Frenchy in the 1950s-set film *Grease*).
20. Pinky Tuscadero (Roz Kelly) almost got him to the altar. Fonzie decided she was too famous, though (she was a singer about to appear on *The Ed Sullivan Show*), and he didn't want to be known as "Mr. Pinky Tuscadero."

I Dream of Jeannie

1965–70, starring Barbara Eden, Larry Hagman, Bill Daily, Hayden Rorke

1. How did Tony Nelson happen to be on the island where he found Jeannie in her bottle, on the first episode?
2. Who had placed Jeannie in the bottle, and why did he do it?
3. Who played the character named in the previous question? How was this actor related to Barbara Eden?
4. How old was Jeannie when Tony found her?
5. Where did Tony work?
6. On the first few episodes, Tony was engaged to a general's daughter—but of course Jeannie threw a monkey wrench into that engagement. Name the fiancée.
7. Who, besides Tony, knew Jeannie was a genie?
8. What was the name of the devious, dark-haired genie also played by Barbara Eden?
9. What was the name of Jeannie's dog?
10. What was the name of Dr. Bellows' wife?
11. What future star of *Charlie's Angels* played Roger's girlfriend, Tina, during *I Dream of Jeannie's* final season?
12. What color was Jeannie's harem costume in almost all the episodes?
13. In the first *Jeannie* TV reunion movie, *I Dream of Jeannie: 15 Years Later*, which former star of *M*A*S*H* took over the role of Tony?
14. In the 1991 TV movie reunion *I Still Dream of Jeannie*, Tony was off in space on a special mission and thus unseen. In order to remain in the U.S., Jeannie was forced to find a temporary master, and she settled on a high school guidance counselor. Which one of Larry Hagman's former *Dallas* costars played Jeannie's temporary master?
15. In *I Still Dream of Jeannie*, the Nelsons had a teenaged son. What was his name?
16. What prolific author created *I Dream of Jeannie*?
17. What other classic TV series did Bill Daily star on, as an airline pilot?

I Dream of Jeannie—Answers

1. When his space mission was aborted, he was forced to parachute to safety, and he landed on the island.
2. When Jeannie refused to marry an evil genie called The Blue Djin, he turned her into a genie and put her in the bottle.
3. Michael Ansara was Barbara Eden's husband at the time.
4. 2,000
5. At NASA in Cocoa Beach, Florida.
6. Melissa was played by Karen Sharpe.
7. Tony's best friend Roger Healy (Bill Daily) knew the secret.
8. Her name was also Jeannie.
9. Gin-Gin
10. Amanda
11. Farrah Fawcett (before she was Farrah Fawcett-Majors)
12. Pink
13. Wayne Rogers
14. Ken Kercheval
15. Tony Nelson Jr.
16. Sidney Sheldon, who also created *Hart to Hart*
17. *The Bob Newhart Show*

I Love Lucy

1951–57, starring Lucille Ball, Desi Arnaz, Vivian Vance, William Frawley

1. What was Lucy's maiden name?
2. What was Ricky's native country?
3. At which musical instrument did Little Ricky excel?
4. What caped super hero swooped into a 1957 episode?
5. On a very popular series of episodes, the Ricardos and Mertzes traveled to Hollywood, because Ricky was starring in a movie. What was the name of the movie? And what hotel did they stay in?
6. Which Marx Brother did Lucy impersonate while they were in Hollywood?
7. Whose footprints did Lucy and Ethel swipe from the sidewalk in front of Grauman's Chinese Theater?
8. What type of food did Lucy smuggle from Europe, disguised as a baby, in the episode "Return Home From Europe"?
9. What was Ethel's hometown? What was her maiden name?
10. Name Lucille Ball and Desi Arnaz's two real-life children.
11. Was Little Ricky played by Lucy and Desi's real-life son?
12. What was the name of Ricky's signature song?
13. What Connecticut town did the Ricardos move to in 1957?
14. What future film star played a teenage boy smitten with Lucy in the episode "The Young Fans"?
15. What talented blonde actress who later went on to star in her own magical sitcom made one of her first TV appearances in the 1957 episode "Country Club Dance"?
16. Who was older, Fred or Ricky?
17. What was the product (which was mostly alcohol) that Lucy endorsed in a commercial on live TV (getting drunk, as she took doses)?
18. Which family-oriented show did William Frawley (Fred Mertz) later star on, as Uncle Bub?

19. Near the end of her career, Vivian Vance had a role in a series of TV commercials. What type of office worker did she portray?

20. What was the name of the production company Lucille and Desi formed, incorporating parts of each of their names?

I Love Lucy—Answers

1. Lucille MacGillicuddy
2. Cuba
3. Drums
4. Superman, played by George Reeves (who also portrayed the Man of Steel on the 1950s series *Adventures of Superman*), landed next to Lucy on the ledge outside her apartment in the episode "Lucy and Superman." She'd been pretending to be Superman, to entertain the children at Little Ricky's birthday party. Also guest-starring on this episode was Madge Blake, who would later play Aunt Harriett on *Batman*.
5. The movie was *Don Juan*; they stayed at the Beverly Palms Hotel.
6. Lucy and Harpo Marx performed an elaborate mirror routine, inspired by a similar stunt he'd done in one of the Marx Brothers films, *Duck Soup* (1933).
7. John Wayne in the 1955 episode "Lucy and John Wayne"
8. Cheese—a gift for her mother. Her seatmate on the plane was played by Mary Jane Croft.
9. Albuquerque, New Mexico; Ethel Mae Potter
10. Desi and Lucie Arnaz.
11. No. Richard Keith (a.k.a. Keith Thibodeaux) played Little Ricky in the 1956–57 season.
12. *Babalu*
13. Westport
14. Richard Crenna played Arthur.
15. Barbara Eden, who went on to headline *I Dream of Jeannie*, played the center of attention at a country club dance on the aptly titled episode. Her character's name was Diana Jordan.
16. Fred
17. Vita-meata-vegamin
18. Frawley appeared on *My Three Sons* from 1960 to 1965.
19. Vance played Maxine, a coffee hostess, pushing a cart of Maxwell House Coffee.
20. They founded Desilu, which went on to produce such classics as *Star Trek*.

Laverne & Shirley

1976–83, starring Penny Marshall, Cindy Williams

1. What was the show's theme song?
2. Where did the girls work and what did they do there?
3. Which *Happy Days* star guest-starred in the second episode, "The Bachelor Party"?
4. How did Laverne customize all of her blouses?
5. What was the name of Shirley's stuffed cat?
6. What was Laverne's favorite beverage?
7. The girls played hookers in an Army training film. What was the film called?
8. What were the nicknames of the girls' wacky male neighbors?
9. In later episodes, the girls' landlady was married to Laverne's dad. Name the character and the actress.
10. Who guest-starred as Shirley's brother, Bobby?
11. Where did the girls move in the sixth season?
12. Laverne's dad owned two different restaurants at various times on the series. Name them both.
13. What was Carmine's nickname for Shirley?
14. Which star of the film *Star Wars* guest-starred in the episode "The Playboy Show," in which Laverne tried to become a Playboy Bunny?
15. Which girl married a doctor (in the episode "The Mummy's Bride") and abruptly left the show?
16. In the final episode, Carmine moved to New York and got a part in a Broadway play. What was the show?

Laverne and Shirley—**Answers**

1. "Making Our Dreams Come True"
2. They were bottle-cappers at the Shotz Brewery in Milwaukee.
3. She attached a large letter "L" to them.
4. Boo-Boo Kitty
5. Milk and Pepsi
6. *This Can Happen to You*
7. Lenny and Squiggy, played by Michael McKean and David L. Lander
8. Edna Babish, played by stage and screen veteran Betty Garrett
9. Ed Begley Jr.
10. Los Angeles
11. In Milwaukee, he owned The Pizza Bowl; in California it was Cowboy Bill's Western Grub.
12. Angel Face
14. Carrie Fisher (Princess Leia in *Star Wars*)
15. Shirley
16. *Hair*

The Mary Tyler Moore Show

1970–77, starring Mary Tyler Moore, Ed Asner, Ted Knight

1. What city was the setting of *The Mary Tyler Moore Show* (*MTMS*)?
2. What was the last name of Mary's coworker, Murray?
3. What was Murray's job?
4. What was the name of Ted Baxter's girlfriend (eventually his wife)?
5. What color did Ted's wife choose for her wedding dress?
6. Name all three spin-offs of *MTMS*.
7. Mary and Rhoda reunited for a 2000 TV movie. Name it.
8. Who played sex-crazed Sue Ann Nivens?
9. What was Sue Ann's job?
10. Sue Ann had an affair with the husband of one of Mary's friends. Which friend, and what was the name of the husband?
11. Did Mary live in the same apartment throughout the entire run of the series?
12. On what many consider the series' finest half-hour, "Chuckles Bites the Dust," Chuckles the clown met a tragic end. How was Chuckles killed?
13. What was Chuckles' credo, recited seriously by Ted Baxter on his newscast after Chuckles' death?
14. In the final episode of *MTMS*, all but one member of the news team was fired. Who was spared?
15. On what earlier TV classic did Mary Tyler Moore star as the wife of a comedy writer?
16. What were the call letters of the television station where Mary and company worked?
17. Which *MTMS* cast member went on to play the captain of *The Love Boat*?
18. What symbolic gesture did Mary make at the end of the opening credits?
19. In the first episode, Lou Grant said he didn't like one of Mary's traits, during her job interview. What trait was it?
20. What wooden letter hung on the wall of Mary's apartment?
21. What *Match Game* star guest-starred as Rhoda's Aunt Rose in the episode "Rhoda's Sister Gets Married"?

22. What real-life newsman showed up at the TV station to visit Lou on a 1974 episode, prompting Ted to assume (incorrectly) that he was being recruited for the big time?

23. What was the name of the news show anchored by Ted Baxter?

24. What medical emergency served as a wake-up call to Ted, in the episode "Ted's Change of Heart"?

25. In the episode "Mary and the Sexagenarian," Mary briefly dated the father of one of the show's main characters. Which character?

26. In the next-to-last episode of the series, Mary went on a date with someone she'd thus far only considered a friend. Who was he, and what was the outcome of the date?

27. How did the very last scene of the series end?

The Mary Tyler Moore Show—**Answers**

1. Minneapolis
2. Slaughter
3. News writer
4. Georgette Franklin
5. Ted's favorite color, plaid
6. *Rhoda*, *Phyllis*, and *Lou Grant* (Betty White did go on to *The Betty White Show*, but she didn't play Sue Ann Nivens.)
7. *Mary & Rhoda*
8. Betty White
9. Hostess of *The Happy Homemaker Show*
10. Her fling was with Phyllis' husband, Lars.
11. No. She moved into a new place during the show's sixth season, in 1975.
12. Dressed in a peanut costume, he was attacked by a rampaging elephant.
13. "A little song, a little dance, a little seltzer down your pants."
14. Ted Baxter
15. Mary played Laura Petrie on *The Dick Van Dyke Show*.
16. WJM-TV
17. Gavin MacLeod
18. She tossed her hat in the air.
19. He hated her "spunk."
20. An "M"
21. Brett Somers
22. Walter Cronkite
23. *The Six O'Clock News*
24. He had a mild heart attack while on the air.
25. She went out with Murray's father, Doug Booth, played by Lew Ayres.
26. She went out with her boss, Lou Grant in "Lou Dates Mary." They realized by episode's end that they'd never be more than friends.
27. Mary turned out the lights in the newsroom and closed the door.

M*A*S*H

1. What is the title of the show's theme song?
2. Which actor was the only one who appeared in both the TV series and the film that inspired it?
3. What was the M*A*S*H's unit number?
4. What did the acronym M*A*S*H stand for?
5. In early episodes, what did Max Klinger do, in an attempt to get discharged from the Army?
6. What was Hawkeye's hometown?
7. Who went home first, Trapper John or B.J.?
8. Why did Frank Burns leave Korea?
9. What was Margaret Houlihan's nickname?
10. Before Harry Morgan joined the cast fulltime as Col. Potter, what part did he play in an earlier appearance on *M*A*S*H*?
11. What was the name of Col. Potter's stateside wife?
12. In early episodes, an African-American character had a very politically incorrect name. What was it?
13. Name *M*A*S*H*'s two sequels/spin-offs.
14. Which *M*A*S*H* alum played a hotel manager in *Checking In*, the short-lived spin-off of *The Jeffersons*?
15. What was the nickname of the tent where Hawkeye and his tent mates lived?
16. Which real-life relative of series star Alan Alda guest-starred on two episodes as a heart surgeon with a drinking problem?
17. What sad event happened after Henry Blake finally got discharged and sent home?
18. What was the name of B.J. Hunnicutt's stateside wife?
19. Which actor donned a wig to play his character's mother in the episode "Mail Call, Again"?
20. What was Radar's favorite soft drink?
21. Name the camp chaplain.

22. What former football star and movie Tarzan played Margaret's husband, Donald Penobscott? (He was the second actor to play Donald.)
23. What city was Max Klinger from?

M*A*S*H—Answers

1. "Suicide is Painless." A character in the film version sang its lyrics, but it was strictly instrumental on the TV series.

2. Gary Burghoff (Radar)

3. 4077th

4. Mobile Army Surgical Hospital

5. He wore women's clothing, in an attempt to get a "section eight" discharge. Eventually, the sight gag wore thin, and the writers found other funny things for Klinger to do.

6. Crabapple Cove, Maine

7. Trapper John

8. After his girlfriend, Margaret, got married, he lost his mind.

9. Hotlips

10. He guest-starred as a senile general named Bartford Hamilton Steele in a 1974 episode titled "The General Flipped at Dawn." He won an Emmy for that appearance.

11. Mildred

12. Spearchucker

13. *AfterMASH* followed the adventures of Col. Potter, Klinger, and Father Mulcahy when they returned to the United States. It only lasted a little more than a year. *Trapper John, M.D.* fared better; the hour-long drama lasted seven years (1979–86).

14. Larry Linville

15. The Swamp

16. Alan's father, Robert Alda, played Dr. Anthony Borelli.

17. He died when his plane was shot down over the Sea of Japan, before he reached home, in the 1975 episode "Abyssinia, Henry."

18. Peg

19. Gary Burghoff played Mrs. O'Reilly.

20. Grape Nehi

21. Father Francis Mulcahy

22. Mike Henry (star of *Tarzan and the Great River*, with classic TV actress Diana Millay)

23. Toldeo, Ohio

Moonlighting

1985–89, starring Cybill Shepherd, Bruce Willis, Allyce Beasley, Curtis Armstrong

1. In the first episode, a dying man spit out something and presented it to Maddie, setting her off on her first detective case. What was it?

2. What did Maddie do for a living before becoming a detective?

3. In the episode "Brother, Can You Spare a Blonde?" David's brother showed up and romanced Maddie. Name the brother and the actor who played him.

4. What legendary actor/director performed the introduction to the 1985 episode "The Dream Sequence Always Rings Twice" and then died a few days before the episode was broadcast?

5. Which Shakespeare play was parodied in the 1986 episode "Atomic Shakespeare"?

6. In the 1986 Christmas episode, "It's a Wonderful Job," Maddie saw what would have happened if she had sold the detective agency instead of joining it. In this alternate universe, what mystery-solving husband-and-wife team from another ABC series took over the Blue Moon office space?

7. Where did Maddie go to sort out her feelings when she discovered she was pregnant in the show's fourth season?

8. Name the character Maddie met aboard a train and briefly married—and the actor who played him.

9. Who was the father of Maddie's baby, and how did her pregnancy end?

10. Which supporting characters were the focus of the episode "Here's Living With You, Kid"?

11. Who played Miss DiPesto's mom in the episode "Los Dos DiPestos"?

12. How was Maddie related to Annie (Virginia Madsen), with whom David had a brief fling in the series' final season?

13. In the episode "When Girls Collide," David was smitten with a lovely woman he saw in an elevator. Who played her?

14. What song was heard as David and Maddie finally made love in the 1987 episode "I Am Curious…Maddie"?

15. Who sang *Moonlighting*'s theme song?

16. What cameo role did Allyce Beasley play in the 2001 film *Legally Blonde*?

17. In what action movie series did Bruce Willis play wisecracking cop John McClane?

18. Which spooky 1999 Bruce Willis film featured a child who uttered the famous line, "I see dead people!"? Who played the kid?

19. What manic homemaking TV host did Cybill Shepherd play in a "based-on-a-true-story" TV movie in 2003?

20. What was the occupation of Cybill's character in her 1995–98 sitcom *Cybill*?

Moonlighting—**Answers**

1. A wristwatch
2. She was a model.
3. Richard Addison was played by Charles Rocket.
4. Orson Wells
5. *Taming of the Shrew*, with Bruce Willis as Petruchio and Cybill Shepherd as Kate
6. *Hart to Hart*'s Jonathan and Jennifer ran Hart Investigations there. (It was a clever nod to the fact that *Hart to Hart* had previously aired during the *Moonlighting* timeslot.)
7. She fled to her parents' home in Chicago.
8. Walter Bishop, played by Dennis Dugan
9. In the episode "Womb With a View," it was revealed that David was the baby's father, and by the end of the episode, she had miscarried.
10. Bert Viola and Agnes DiPesto took center stage. Series stars Willis and Shepherd, famously feuding with their bosses and with each other, did not appear in this episode.
11. Imogene Coca
12. They were cousins.
13. Bruce Willis' real-life wife, Demi Moore
14. "Be My Baby," by the Ronettes
15. Al Jarreau
16. She played Elle Woods' college counselor, who was bemused when seemingly ditzy Elle expressed a desire to attend Harvard Law School.
17. The *Die Hard* movies, starting in 1988
18. *The Sixth Sense*; Haley Joel Osment
19. She played the title role in *Martha Inc.: The Story of Martha Stewart.*
20. In *Cybill*, beautiful, middle-aged actress Cybill played beautiful, middle-aged actress Cybill.

Mork & Mindy

1978–82, starring Robin Williams, Pam Dawber

1. What was the shape of the spaceship that carried Mork from his home planet of Ork to Earth?
2. What was the primary difference between Mork and other Orkans?
3. What job was Mork sent to Earth to do?
4. In the first episode, Mork told Mindy about a blind date he had with someone during his previous visit to Earth. Who was the date, and who played her?
5. What kind of store did Mindy's dad own and operate in early episodes?
6. What was Mindy's grandma's name, and who played her?
7. In later episodes, Mindy became the host of a morning TV show. Name it.
8. What was the name of Mindy's mom (who died many years before Mork arrived on Earth)?
9. In the episode "A Mommy for Mindy," Mindy's dad married a younger woman named Cathy. Name the actress, who had a hit single in 1962 called "Johnny Angel."
10. Mork befriended Exidor, an eccentric who claimed he had a group of invisible followers (called the Friends of Venus). Name Exidor's invisible dog.
11. Raquel Welch played Captain Nirvana, an evil alien who captured Mindy in a two-parter called "Mork vs. the Necrotons." What did Nirvana do with the Earthling?
12. Where did Mork and Mindy spend their honeymoon?
13. Who gave birth to Mork and Mindy's son? What was the son's name and who played him?
14. What was unusual about the aging process of Mork and Mindy's son?
15. What was the Orkan greeting phrase?
16. What was the Orkan curse-word?
17. What was the occupation of Mork and Mindy's cranky neighbor, Mr. Bickley?
18. What was the name of Pam (Mindy) Dawber's next sitcom? Why was it cancelled?

19. What was the title of the 1993 film in which Robin Williams played a man posing as a female nanny?

20. Which cast member played himself in one of *The New Scooby-Doo Movies* in 1972?

Mork & Mindy—**Answers**

1. It was egg-shaped.
2. Other Orkans had no senses of humor; Mork did.
3. He was sent to observe Earthling behavior and report back to Orson, leader of Ork.
4. *Laverne and Shirley*'s Laverne, played by Penny Marshall
5. He owned McConnell's Music Store.
6. Cora Hudson was played by Elizabeth Kerr.
7. *Wake Up, Boulder*
8. Beth
9. Shelly Fabares' angelic ditty sold more than a million copies while she was playing teen Mary Stone on *The Donna Reed Show*.
10. Brutus
11. She put Mindy in a big birdcage.
12. Ork
13. Mork laid an egg, which yielded Mearth, played by Jonathan Winters.
14. Mearth aged in reverse; he was born old and grew younger.
15. Na-nu, na-nu
16. Shazbot!
17. He wrote greeting cards.
18. *My Sister Sam* (1986–88) left the air after star Rebecca Schaeffer was murdered by an obsessed fan.
19. *Mrs. Doubtfire*
20. Jonathan Winters

The Munsters

1964–66, starring Yvonne DeCarlo, Fred Gwynne, Al Lewis

1. What was the Munsters' address?
2. What did Herman do for a living?
3. Which family member was recast during the show's first season?
4. What type of monster was Eddie?
5. What was the name of the 1966 feature film based on the show?
6. Was the feature film shot in color or black and white?
7. What was the name of Eddie's pet dragon?
8. Name Herman's twin brother.
9. Where was Grandpa's laboratory?
10. Which former Catwoman assumed the role of Lily when the show was resurrected as *The Munsters Today* in 1988?
11. What type of monster was Lily's brother?
12. What did the kids at school call Eddie in the episode "Eddie's Nickname"?
13. What insult-tossing comedian guest-starred as a dance instructor in the episode "Dance With Me, Herman"?
14. In episode # 44, it was revealed that Herman and Lily had been married a remarkably long time. How long?
15. What caused Herman to lose his memory in the episode "John Doe Munster"?
16. Herman's vampire wife had a different name in the pilot. What was it?
17. In the episode "Just Another Pretty Face," Fred Gwynne played Herman without the monster make-up. Why did Herman look like a normal human in this episode?
18. Was Grandpa's last name Munster?
19. Before they did *The Munsters*, Fred Gwynne and Al Lewis co-starred in another classic sitcom from 1961 to '63. What was the name of the show, and what was the occupation shared by their characters?
20. Which *Munsters* cast member had a role in 1956 film classic *The Ten Commandments*?

The Munsters—**Answers**

1. 1313 Mockingbird Lane
2. He worked in a funeral parlor.
3. Marilyn Munster was played by Beverly Owen, then Pat Priest. Beverly's final episode was # 13, "Family Portrait."
4. A werewolf
5. *Munster, Go Home* (The movie's plot: The Munsters traveled to England, where Herman had inherited a castle called Munster Hall. The British branch of the family was less than welcoming.)
6. Unlike the TV series, which was shot in black-and-white, the movie was filmed in color.
7. Spot
8. Herman's twin, Charlie, appeared in the episode "Knock Wood, Here Comes Charlie."
9. His lab was in the basement, accessed through a trapdoor.
10. Lee Meriwether
11. A wolfman
12. Shorty
13. Don Rickles played Happy Havemayer
14. The episode title says it all: "Happy 100th Anniversary."
15. A safe fell on his head.
16. Phoebe
17. He was struck by lightning.
18. No. He was Lily's dad, so he wasn't a Munster. His last name (and Lily's maiden name) was Dracula.
19. In *Car 54, Where Are You?*, they played New York cops.
20. Yvonne De Carlo played Sephora.

The Odd Couple

1970–73, starring Jack Klugman, Tony Randall

1. What former *Father Knows Best* daughter played one of Felix's girlfriends, Miriam Welby?

2. What future movie director played Oscar's secretary, Myrna Tuner?

3. What was Oscar's occupation?

4. One of the boys' poker buddies was a public servant named Murray. What was his job?

5. In a 1973 episode, Felix and Oscar won a big prize on a radio quiz show. What was the prize?

6. In a 1972 episode, Felix pestered Oscar to appear on a popular game show with him. Which show?

7. The next year, the boys went on another game show, hosted by Monty Hall, who guest-starred as himself. Name the show and you'll name the episode as well.

8. What feuding tennis stars played themselves in "The Pig Who Came to Dinner"?

9. *The Odd Couple* was based on a Neil Simon play of the same name. Who played the boys in the 1968 film based on the play?

10. What wisecracking game show star played Oscar's ex-wife, Blanche?

11. What was the name of Felix's ex-wife?

12. What happened in the final episode?

13. Jack Klugman went on to play a crime-solving medical examiner in his own dramatic series. Name it.

14. Tony Randall starred in a situation comedy with Swoozie Kurtz from 1981 to '83. Name it.

The Odd Couple—**Answers**

1. Eleanor Donahue played Miriam Welby.

2. Penny Marshall, director of such films as *A League of Their Own*, played Myrna.

3. He was a sportswriter for the fictional newspaper *The New York Herald*.

4. An NYPD cop

5. The episode was titled "The New Car." Dick Clark guest-starred as himself.

6. The episode was titled "*Password*." Host Allen Ludden and his wife, Betty White, guest-starred as themselves.

7. "*Let's Make a Deal*." The boys were in costume together as a horse.

8. Bobby Riggs and Billy Jean King. (The episode title was a reference to the fact that Billy often called Bobby a male chauvinist pig.)

9. Walter Matthau and Jack Lemmon

10. *Match Game* staple Brett Somers

11. Gloria

12. In "Felix Remarries," Felix and Gloria reunited.

13. *Quincy*

14. *Love, Sidney*

The Patty Duke Show

1963–66, starring Patty Duke, William Schallert, Jean Byron

1. Fill in the blank, from the show's theme song: "But Patty's only seen the sights
_____."
2. Were Patty and Cathy twin sisters?
3. Name the family dog.
4. What was the name of the book written by Patty?
5. Name Patty's boyfriend
6. Who played Cathy's dad?
7. What was the name of the malt shop where the girls hung out?
8. What was Martin Lane's job?
9. Name Patty's little brother.
10 What musical instrument did Patty try to learn to play in the episode "Practice Makes Perfect"?
11. Patty Duke played yet another role in the episode "The Perfect Hostess." Whom did she play?
12. Two members of the Rat Pack guest starred in a 1965 episode. Name them.
13. What was the occupation of the character played by Troy Donahue, whom Patty fell for in a 1965 episode?
14. What teen heartthrob dropped by the Lane household, kicking off the third and final season in the 1965 episode "A Foggy Day in Brooklyn Heights"?
15. What novelty song about an oft-married woman did Patty sing in the 1965 episode "Partying is Such Sweet Sorrow"?
16. In what 1967 film did Patty Duke play a drug-addled singer named Neely O'Hara?
17. For what 1962 film did Patty Duke win an Oscar, playing Helen Keller?
18. What was the name of the 1999 TV movie reunion of *The Patty Duke Show*?
19. Which member of *The Addams Family* was Patty Duke married to, from 1972 to '85. What was her professional name at the time?
20. What son of sitcom "royalty" did Patty Date before marrying the man named in # 19?

The Patty Duke Show—**Answers**

1. "...a girl can see from Brooklyn Heights."
2. No, they're identical cousins.
3. Tiger
4. *I Was a Teenage Teenager*
5. Richard Harrison
6. William Schallert played the twin fathers of Cathy and Patty.
7. In early episodes it was called the Shake Shop; in later episodes it was Leslie's Ice Cream Parlor.
8. He was managing editor of *The New York Chronicle* newspaper.
9. Ross, played by Paul O'Keefe
10. The tuba
11. Cousin Betsy, a Southern belle from Chattanooga
12. Sammy Davis Jr. and Peter Lawford appeared in "Will the Real Sammy Davis Please Hang Up?"
13. Troy played a doctor in "Operation: Tonsils."
14. Frankie Avalon. He also appeared in a dream sequence in the show's 12th episode, "How to Be Popular."
15. "Henry the Eighth," a song about a man who is a woman's eight husband named Henry. Patty sang it in first person ("I'm Henry the Eight, I am, I am...")
16. *Valley of the Dolls*
17. *The Miracle Worker*
18. *The Patty Duke Show: Still Rockin' in Brooklyn Heights* (The plot: The gang rallies around Patty as she fights to keep her old high school from being torn down.)
19. While married to John Astin (Gomez), she used the professional name Patty Duke Astin.
20. She dated Desi Arnaz Jr., son of Desi Arnaz and Lucille Ball. Lucy was reported to be less than thrilled that her son was dating the wild-acting older woman.

Petticoat Junction

1963–70, starring Bea Benadaret, Edgar Buchanan, Meredith MacRae

1. What was the name of the hotel run by Kate Bradley, where this series took place?
2. Name Kate Bradley's three daughters.
3. Which daughter was oldest?
4. Was Kate divorced or widowed?
5. What type of pet did the girls have?
6. How did crop-duster pilot Steve Elliott meet the Bradleys? Which daughter eventually married him?
7. Where did the Elliotts honeymoon?
8. What was the Elliotts' daughter's name?
9. Which of *The Beverley Hillbillies* briefly comes to the Shady Rest to help care for the Elliotts' new baby?
10. How was actress Linda Kaye related to the show's producer, Paul Henning?
11. After Bea Benadaret (Kate) died, which character took Kate's place as surrogate mother to the three girls? Who played her?
12. Name the train that linked Kate's hotel with the rest of the world.
13. Name the train's engineer and its conductor.
14. What was "Pixley"?
15. In the episode "My Daughter the Doctor," what did Billie Jo want to do when she received a $500 insurance payment?
16. What was the name of the singing group the girls briefly formed?
17. What was the name of Kate's archenemy, played first by Virginia Sale, then by Elvia Allman.
18. Who played a handsome male doctor visiting Dr. Janet Craig in the series next-to-last episode, "No, No, You Can't Take Her Away"?

Petticoat Junction—**Answers**

1. The Shady Rest Hotel
2. Billie Jo, Bobbie Jo, and Betty Jo
3. Billie Jo
4. Widowed
5. A dog
6. He crashed his plane outside Hooterville when he saw the girls swimming in the town water tower, and the girls nursed him back to health. Eventually he and Betty Jo tied the knot.
7. Hawaii
8. Kathy Jo
9. Granny (Irene Ryan). (She ended up caring for the family dog when she lost her glasses and couldn't tell the dog from the infant.)
10. She was his daughter.
11. Dr. Janet Craig, played by June Lockhart
12. The Cannonball Express
13. Engineer: Charley Pratt; Conductor: Floyd Smoot
14. A town near Hooterville
15. Billie Jo wanted to go to Hollywood to become an actress.
16. The Lady Bugs
17. Selma Plout
18. Keith Andes played Dr. Marlowe.

Saturday Night Live

1975 to present

Name the series regulars who played the following recurring characters:

1. Roseanne Rosannadanna
2. Tom Snyder
3. Gerald Ford
4. The Church Lady
5. Ed Grimley
6. Pat Stevens
7. Mango
8. Cheerleader Craig
9. Dr. Ruth
10. The Samurai
11. Stuart Smalley
12. The Sweeney Sisters
13. Pathological Liar Tommy Flanagan
14. Master Thespian
15. Fernando
16. Wayne Campbell
17. Connie Conehead
18. Opera Man
19. Gumby
20. Donatella Versace
21. Mary Katherine Gallagher
22. Pat
23. The Blues Brothers

Saturday Night Live—Answers

1. Gilda Radner
2. Dan Aykroyd
3. Chevy Chase
4. Dana Carvey
5. Martin Short
6. Nora Dunn
7. Chris Kattan
8. Will Farrell
9. Mary Gross
10. John Belushi
11. Al Franken
12. Jan Hooks and Nora Dunn
13. Jon Lovitz
14. Jon Lovitz
15. Billy Crystal
16. Mike Myers
17. Laraine Newman
18. Adam Sandler
19. Eddie Murphy
20. Maya Rudolph
21. Molly Shannon
22. Julia Sweeney
23. Dan Aykroyd and John Belushi

The Simpsons

1989 to present, starring Julie Kavner, Dan Castellaneta, Nancy Cartwright, Yeardley Smith

1. Before getting a show of their own, the Simpson characters were featured in animated shorts during another show. What was it?
2. What was Marge's maiden name?
3. What was the name of the shop run by Apu?
4. Name Bart's grade-school teacher.
5. What did bumbling lazybones Homer do for a living?
6. What musical instrument did Lisa play?
7. Name the Simpson kids, in age order, oldest to youngest.
8. Who voiced Ms. Botz, the Babysitter Bandit, in the episode "Some Enchanted Evening"?
9. What comic book character was Bart's favorite?
10. In the episode "Stark Raving Dad," what happened to Homer after he wore a pink shirt to work?
11. What was the name of the Simpsons' dog?
12. What job did Homer take on in the episode "Colonel Homer"?
13. What did Homer give Marge for her 34th birthday in the episode "Life in the Fast Lane"?
14. Who voiced Homer's male secretary, Karl, in the episode "Simpson and Delilah"?
15. What violet-eyed beauty provided Maggie's voice for the episode "Maggie's First Word"?
16. What color was Marge's hair?
17. The episode "Simpsoncalifragilisticexpiala(Annoyed Grunt)cious" was a parody of *Mary Poppins*. What was the name of the Simpsons' magical nanny?
18. Who created *The Simpsons*? What edgy comic strip did he create earlier, which featured some characters greatly resembling some of the Simpsons?

The Simpsons—Answers

1. *The Tracey Ullman Show.* Series regulars Julie Kavner and Dan Castellaneta leant their voices to Marge and Homer, probably never dreaming that their *Simpsons* work would not only outlive their *Tracey Ullman Show* gig (the show ran from 1987 to '90), but would continue more than another decade.

2. Marjorie Bouvier (just like Jackie Kennedy)

3. the Qwik-E-Mart

4. Edna Krabappel

5. He was the safety inspector at a nuclear power plant.

6. The saxophone

7. Bart, Lisa, Maggie

8. Penny Marshall

9. Radioactive Man

10. He was committed to a mental institution, where his roommate was a big white man who thought he was Michael Jackson.

11. Santa's Little Helper

12. He was the manager of a country singer named Lurleen (voiced by Beverly D'Angelo).

13. A bowling ball

14. Harvey Fierstein

15. Elizabeth Taylor

16. Blue

17. Shary Bobbins

18. Matt Groening; Life in Hell

Star Trek

1966–69, starring William Shatner, Leonard Nimoy, DeForest Kelley

1. Who played Captain Christopher Pike in the *Star Trek* pilot, "The Cage"?

2. Who was the only character from "The Cage" to make it into the series?

3. What type of tiny, furry creatures plagued Kirk and his crew in an amusing 1967 episode?

4. What was Mr. Spock's native planet? What color was his blood?

5. What planet was Mr. Spock's mother from? Who played her?

6. What small space vehicle did the Enterprise crew use?

7. What future *Dynasty* star played one of Captain Kirk's most serious lady loves, Edith Keeler, in the award-winning episode "City on the Edge of Forever"? How did she die in the episode?

8. What future star of the film *M*A*S*H* guest-starred in the second *Star Trek* pilot, "Where No Man Has Gone Before," as Dr. Elizabeth Dehner?

9. What actress played Yeoman Janice Rand, a character with a distinctive basket-weave hairstyle?

10. Which cast member was married to *Star Trek* creator Gene Roddenberry?

11. Which villain from the 1967 episode "The Space Seed" returned to battle Kirk in the 1982 film, *Star Trek II*?

12. How many episodes of *Star Trek* are there?

13. What future co-star of the film *Tootsie* guest-starred in the *Star Trek* episode "Assignment Earth"?

14. Which *Star Trek* cast member hosted *Saturday Night Live* in 1986 and appeared in a sketch in which he implored Trekkies to "Get a life!"?

15. Who provided the voice for the Enterprise's computer?

16. What was the title of Leonard Nimoy's 1976 autobiography?

17. Which *Star Trek* cast mates performed TV's first interracial kiss?

18. Who played Commodore Matthew Decker, the crazed starship captain who committed suicide in the episode "The Doomsday Machine"?

19. Who directed the first film based on the TV series, *Star Trek: The Motion Picture* (1979)?

20. Which future star of *Cheers* played a Vulcan in the 1982 film *Star Trek II*?

21. Which *Star Trek* cast member directed the 1989 film *Star Trek V: The Final Frontier*?

Star Trek—**Answers**

1. Jeffrey Hunter, star of such films as *King of Kings* (1961), played Pike.
2. Mr. Spock. (Majel Barrett was also in the pilot and the series, but she played two different characters.)
3. Tribbles, in "The Trouble With Tribbles"
4. Vulcan; green
5. Earth. Jane Wyatt, the mother from *Father Knows Best*, played Spock's mom in a couple of episodes and in the film *Star Trek IV*.
6. A shuttlecraft
7. Joan Collins
8. Sally Kellerman played Elizabeth. Her boyfriend was played by *2001: A Space Odyssey* star Gary Lockwood.
9. Grace Lee Whitney, who later authored a tell-all titled *The Longest Trek: My Tour of the Galaxy*, played Captain Kirk's yeoman.
10. Majel Barrett (Christine Chappel) became Majel Barrett Roddenberry in December 1969.
11. Khan (Ricardo Montalban)
12. 80
13. Terri Garr played a scatterbrained secretary in the episode, which was set on present-day Earth. It was a pilot that wasn't picked up.
14. William Shatner
15. Majel Barrett
16. *I Am Not Spock*
17. William Shatner and Nichelle Nichols (Captain Kirk and Lieutenant Uhura) locked lips in the 1968 episode "Plato's Stepchildren."
18. William Windom
19. Robert Wise, director of such classics as *West Side Story* and *The Sound of Music*, helmed the film.
20. Kirstie Alley
21. William Shatner

Taxi

1978–83, starring Judd Hirsch, Marilu Henner, Danny DeVito, Jeff Conaway, Tony Danza, Christopher Lloyd

1. What was the name of the cab company?
2. What New York City borough was the setting of the show?
3. What was the dispatcher's name, and who played him?
4. Which cabbie was an aspiring actor?
5. What was Alex's last name?
6. Name Elaine Nardo's two kids.
7. What sport did Tony Banta compete in?
8. Danny DeVito's wife guest-starred as Louie's girlfriend, a candy vending machine delivery woman. Name the character and the actress.
9. What *Mary Hartman, Mary Hartman* star guest-starred as Alex's ex-wife, Phyllis?
10. What zany immigrant did Andy Kaufman play? Who played his wife, Simka?
11. Taxi driving was only one of Elaine's jobs. What else did she do for a living?
12. What was the name of Alex's blind date in the show's third episode, "Blind Date"? Hint: Her name was also the title of the show's instrumental theme.
13. What kind of animal was Jim's pet in the episode "Jim Gets a Pet"?
14. Which future member of *The Simpsons* family played a member of Tony's family in a 1980 episode that won an Emmy for writing?
15. Which two main characters had a very brief sexual fling in Europe in the episode "Vienna Waits"?
16. Which character got a really bad haircut in the episode "The Unkindest Cut"?

Taxi—Answers

1. Sunshine Cab Company
2. Manhattan
3. Louie DePalma was played by Danny DeVito.
4. Bobby Wheeler, played by Jeff Conway (Kenickie in the 1978 film *Grease*)
5. Reiger
6. Jason and Jennifer
7. He was a boxer.
8. Rhea Pearlman (Carla on *Cheers*) played Zina Sherman.
9. Louise Lasser
10. Latka's wife was played by Carol Kane.
11. She was a receptionist at an art gallery
12. Angela
13. A horse
14. Julie Kavner, who later voiced Marge Simspon, played Tony's sister, Monica, in "Tony's Sister and Jim."
15. Elaine and Alex.
16. Elaine

Three's Company

1977–84, starring John Ritter, Suzanne Somers, Joyce Dewitt, Audra Lindley, Norman Fell

1. The first episode started with the aftermath of a party (Jack had passed out in the bathtub). What was the purpose of the party?
2. What lie did Janet and Chrissy tell their landlord, so he'd allow a man (Jack) to live with them? Consequently, what was the landlord's *Peter Pan*-inspired nickname for Jack?
3. Where did Jack live before joining the girls?
4. What type of shop did Janet work in?
5. Name the pub where the gang hung out.
6. Name the landlord and his randy wife. What was the name of their spin-off?
7. When the landlords were spun-off, what classic sitcom star played Mr. Furley, who took their place?
8. Which original cast member left the series when producers wouldn't meet her salary demands?
9. What was Chrissy's full name?
10. What was Chrissy's dad's occupation?
11. What did Jack do for a living? What was the name of the business he opened, later in the series?
12. What did Janet accidentally do in the show's opening credits, in early seasons?
13. Who was John Ritter (Jack)'s cowboy-movie-star father?
14. What British series was *Three's Company* based on?
15. When *Three's Company* ended, Jack moved in with his girlfriend on a spin-off. Name it.

Three's Company—**Answers**

1. It was a wedding reception/going-away party for Janet and Chrissy's roommate, a pregnant woman named Eleanor.
2. They told him that Jack was gay. He called Jack "Tinkerbell."
3. The YMCA
4. A flower shop
5. The Regal Beagle
6. Stanley and Helen Roper's series was called *The Ropers*.
7. Don Knotts
8. Suzanne Somers (Chrissy)
9. Christmas Snow
10. He was a minister in Fresno.
11. A chef. He opened Jack's Bistro.
12. While watering a plant, she poured water on Chrissy, who just happened to be wearing a bikini.
13. Tex Ritter
14. *A Man About the House*
15. *Three's A Crowd*

PART III

Places, Names, Songs, and More

Actors
Actresses
Character Names
Jobs
Locales
Networks
Spin-Offs
Theme Songs

Actors

Name the actors who played the following characters:
1. Mike Stivic (*All in the Family*)
2. Jimmy Olsen (*Adventures of Superman*)
3. Dr. McCoy (*Star Trek*)
4. Dr. Bellows (*I Dream of Jeannie*)
5. Fred Mertz (*I Love Lucy*)
6. Gopher (*The Love Boat*)
7. John Boy Walton (*The Waltons*)
8. Matt Dillon (*Gunsmoke*)
9. Bud Anderson (*Father Knows Best*)
10. Bobby Ewing (*Dallas*)
11. Adam Carrington (*Dynasty*)
12. Arthur Carlson (*WKRP in Cincinnati*)
13. Officer Joe Coffey (*Hill Street Blues*)
14. Mr. Sulu (*Star Trek*)
15. Steve Trevor (*Wonder Woman*)
18. Caine (*Kung Fu*)
19. Steve McGarrett (*Hawaii Five-0*)
20. Lt. Bill Crowley (*Police Woman*)
21. Newkirk (*Hogan's Heros*)
22. Carter (*Hogan's Heros*)
23. Mike Brady (*The Brady Bunch*)
24. Bobby Brady (*The Brady Bunch*)
25. Latka (*Taxi*)
26. Police Chief Carl Kanisky (*Gimme a Break*)
27. David Banner (*The Incredible Hulk*)
28. The Hulk (*The Incredible Hulk*)
29. Galen (*Planet of the Apes*)
30. Tommy Hyatt (*Alice*)
31. Buck Rogers (*Buck Rogers in the 25th Century*)
32. Logan 5 (*Logan's Run*)

33. Marcus Welby (*Marcus Welby, M.D.*)
34. George Jefferson (*The Jeffersons*)
35. Harry Bentley (*The Jeffersons*)
36. Barnabas Collins (*Dark Shadows*)
37. Roger Collins (*Dark Shadows*)
38. Lou Grant (*Lou Grant*)
39. Detective Fish (*Fish*)
40. Barney Miller (*Barney Miller*)
41. Max Klinger (*M*A*S*H*)
42. Dr. Seth Hazlett (*Murder, She Wrote*)
43. Max Smart (*Get Smart*)
44. Sgt. Joe Friday (*Dragnet*)
45. Uncle Joe Carson (*Petticoat Junction*)
46. Oliver Douglas (*Green Acres*)
47. Squiggy (*Laverne & Shirley*)
48. David Addison (*Moonlighting*)
49. Ben Matlock (*Matlock*)
50. James T. West (*The Wild Wild West*)
51. Uncle Bill Davis (*Family Affair*)
52. Stanley Zbornak (*The Golden Girls*)
53. Dan August (*Dan August*)
54. Mike Nelson (*Sea Hunt*)
55. Michael Knight (*Knight Rider*)
56. Sid Fairgate (*Knots Landing*)
57. Corporal Agarn (*F Troop*)
58. Craig Carter (*Here's Lucy*)
59. Phineas Bogg (*Voyagers*)
60. Dan Tanna (*Vegas*)
61. Mel Sharples (*Alice*)
62. Harry Orwell (*Harry-O*)
63. Jonathan Hart (*Hart to Hart*)
64. Max (*Hart to Hart*)
65. Ralph Malph (*Happy Days*)
66. Howard Cunningham (*Happy Days*)
67. Larry Appleton (*Perfect Strangers*)
68. Sheriff Harry S. Truman (*Twin Peaks*)
69. Professor John Robinson (*Lost in Space*)
70. John Bosley (*Charlie's Angels*)

71. Lynn Belvedere (*Mr. Belvedere*)
72. Matt Fielding (*Melrose Place*)
73. Tarzan (*Tarzan* [1966–69 version])
74. The Prisoner (*The Prisoner*)
75. Detective Frank Drebin (*Police Squad*)

Actors—**Answers**

1. Rob Reiner
2. Jack Larson
3. DeForest Kelly
4. Hayden Rorke
5. William Frawley
6. Fred Grandy
7. Richard Thomas
8. James Arness
9. Billy Gray
10. Patrick Duffy
11. Gordon Thomson
12. Gordon Jump
13. Ed Marinaro
14. George Takei
15. Lyle Waggoner
18. David Carradine
19. Jack Lord
20. Earl Holliman
21. Richard Dawson
22. Larry Hovis
23. Robert Reed
24. Mike Lookinland
25. Andy Kaufman
26. Dolph Sweet
27. Bill Bixby
28. Lou Ferrigno
29. Roddy McDowall
30. Philip McKeon
31. Gil Gerard
32. Gregory Harrison
33. Robert Young
34. Sherman Hemsley
35. Paul Benedict
36. Jonathan Frid (1966–71 version); Ben Cross (1991 version)
37. Louis Edmonds (1966–71 version); Roy Thinnes (1991 version)
38. Ed Asner

39. Abe Vigoda
40. Hal Linden
41. Jamie Farr
42. William Windom
43. Don Adams
44. Jack Webb
45. Edgar Buchanan
46. Eddie Albert
47. David L. Lander
48. Bruce Willis
49. Andy Griffith
50. Robert Conrad
51. Brian Keith
52. Herb Edelman
53. Burt Reynolds
54. Lloyd Bridges (1957–61 version); Ron Ely (1987–88 version)
55. David Hasselhoff
56. Don Murray
57. Larry Storch
58. Desi Arnaz, Jr.
59. Jon-Erik Hexum
60. Robert Urich
61. Vic Tayback
62. David Janssen
63. Robert Wagner
64. Lionel Stander
65. Donny Most
66. Tom Bosley
67. Mark Linn-Baker
68. Michael Ontkean
69. Guy Williams
70. David Doyle
71. Christopher Hewett
72. Doug Savant
73. Ron Ely
74. Patrick McGoohan
75. Leslie Neilsen

Actresses

Name the actresses who played the following characters:
1. Lily Munster (*The Munsters*)
2. Alice Nelson (*The Brady Bunch*)
3. Della Street (*Perry Mason*)
4. Hazel Burke (*Hazel*)
5. Lovey Howell (*Gilligan's Island*)
6. Marion Cunningham (*Happy Days*)
7. Carol Post (*Mr. Ed*)
8. Esmeralda (*Bewitched*)
9. Alice Mitchell (*Dennis The Menace*)
10. Carol Kester (*The Bob Newhart Show*)
11. Jennifer Marlowe (*WKRP in Cincinnati*)
12. Sammy Jo Carrington (*Dynasty*)
13. Gidget Lawrence (*Gidget*)
14. Margaret "Hotlips" Houlihan (*M*A*S*H*)
15. Mary Beth Lacey (*Cagney & Lacey*)
16. Morticia Addams (*The Addams Family*)
17. Shirley Feeney (*Laverne and Shirley*)
18. Caroline Ingalls (*Little House on the Prairie*)
19. Diana "Wonder Woman" Prince (*Wonder Woman*)
20. Daphne Moon Crane (*Fraiser*)
21. Rhoda (*Rhoda*)
22. Miranda (*Sex and the City*)
23. Helen Crump (*The Andy Griffith Show*)
24. Edwina Monsoon (*Absolutely Fabulous*)
25. Elly May Clampett (*The Beverly Hillbillies*)
26. Granny (*The Beverly Hillbillies*)
27. Kate Bradley (*Petticoat Junction*)
28. Lisa Douglas (*Green Acres*)
29. Mary Stone (*The Donna Reed Show*)
30. Mother Olivia Jefferson (*The Jeffersons*)

31. Helen Willis (*The Jeffersons*)
32. Chrissy Snow (*Three's Company*)
33. Julie Kotter (*Welcome Back, Kotter*)
34. Nurse Dixie McCall (*Emergency!*)
35. Millie Helper (*The Dick Van Dyke Show*)
36. Angelique (*Dark Shadows*)
37. Carolyn Stoddard (*Dark Shadows*)
38. Cindy Brady (*The Brady Bunch*)
39. Sable Colby (*The Colbys*)
40. Elaine Nardo (*Taxi*)
41. Carla Tortelli (*Cheers*)
42. Diane Chambers (*Cheers*)
43. Julia Baker (*Julia*)
44. Sister Bertrille (*The Flying Nun*)
45. Vivian Bagley (*The Lucy Show*)
46. Julie McCoy (*The Love Boat*)
47. Joanie Cunningham (*Joanie Love Chachi*)
48. Suzanne Sugarbaker (*Designing Women*)
49. Mary Jo Shively (*Designing Women*)
50. April Dancer (*The Girl From U.N.C.L.E.*)
51. Florida Evans (*Good Times*)
52. Aunt Esther (*Sanford and Son*)
53. Officer Bonnie Clark (*CHiPs*)
54. Sonny Lumet (*Bosom Buddies*)
55. Kim Carter (*Here's Lucy*)
56. Maureen Robinson (*Lost in Space*)
57. Penny Robinson (*Lost in Space*)
58. Gloria Stivic (*All in the Family*)
59. Kelly Garrett (*Charlie's Angels*)
60. Tiffany Welles (*Charlie's Angels*)
61. Sheriff Hildy Granger (*She's the Sheriff*)
62. Stacey Colbert (*Ned and Stacey*)
63. Judy Benjamin (*Private Benjamin*)
64. Jessica Tate (*Soap*)
65. Corinne Tate (*Soap*)
66. Jennifer Keaton (*Family Ties*)
67. Buffy (*Family Affair*)
68. Buffy (*Buffy the Vampire Slayer*)

69. Aunt Bee Taylor (*The Andy Griffith Show*)
70. Batgirl (*Batman*)
71. Stella Johnson (*Harper Valley PTA*)
72. Agent 99 (*Get Smart*)
73. J.C. Wyatt (*Baby Boom*)
74. Mrs. Amanda King (*Scarecrow and Mrs. King*)
75. Maddie Hayes (*Moonlighting*)

Actresses—Answers

1. Yvonne De Carlo
2. Ann B. Davis
3. Barbara Hale
4. Shirley Booth
5. Natalie Schafer
6. Marion Ross
7. Connie Hines
8. Alice Ghostley
9. Gloria Henry
10. Marcia Wallace
11. Loni Anderson
12. Heather Locklear
13. Sally Field
14. Loretta Swit
15. Tyne Daly
16. Carolyn Jones
17. Cindy Williams
18. Karen Grassle
19. Lynda Carter
20. Jane Leeves
21. Valerie Harper
22. Cynthia Nixon
23. Aneta Corsaut
24. Jennifer Saunders
25. Donna Douglas
26. Irene Ryan
27. Bea Benaderet
28. Eva Gabor
29. Shelley Fabares
30. Zara Cully
31. Roxie Roker
32. Suzanne Somers
33. Marcia Strassman
34. Julie London
35. Ann Morgan Guilbert
36. Lara Parker (1966–71 version); Lysette Anthony (1991 version)

37. Nancy Barrett (1966–71 version); Barbara Blackburn (1991 version)
38. Susan Olsen
39. Stephanie Beacham
40. Marilu Henner
41. Rhea Perlman
42. Shelley Long
43. Diahann Carroll
44. Sally Field
45. Vivian Vance
46. Lauren Tewes
47. Erin Moran
48. Delta Burke
49. Annie Potts
50. Stefanie Powers
51. Esther Rolle
52. LaWanda Page
53. Randi Oakes
54. Donna Dixon
55. Lucie Arnaz
56. June Lockhart
57. Angela Cartwright
58. Sally Struthers
59. Jaclyn Smith
60. Shelley Hack
61. Suzanne Somers
62. Debra Messing
63. Lorna Patterson
64. Katherine Helmond
65. Diana Canova
66. Tina Yothers
67. Anissa Jones
68. Sarah Michelle Gellar
69. Francis Bavier
70. Yvonne Craig
71. Barbara Eden
72. Barbara Feldon
73. Kate Jackson

74. Kate Jackson
75. Cybill Shepherd

Character Names

Provide these characters' last names:

1. Hawkeye _____ (*M*A*S*H*)
2. Ralph_____ (*The Honeymooners*)
3. Maxwell _____ (*Get Smart*)
4. Larry _____ (*Bewitched*)
5. Sabrina _____ (*Charlie's Angels*)
6. Bruce _____ (*Batman*)
7. Ethel _____ (*I Love Lucy*)
8. Howard _____ (*The Andy Griffith Show*)
9. Jethro _____ (*The Beverly Hillbillies*)
10. Bob _____ (*The Bob Newhart Show*)
11. Lumpy _____ (*Leave it to Beaver*)
12. Napoleon _____ (*The Man from U.N.C.L.E.*)
13. Elizabeth _____ (*Dark Shadows*)
14. Phyllis _____ (*The Mary Tyler Moore Show*)
15. Richie _____ (*Happy Days*)
16. Maude _____ (*Maude*)
17. Vinnie _____ (*Welcome Back, Kotter*)
18. Jack _____ (*Three's Company*)
19. Ginger _____ (*Gilligan's Island*)
20. Mindy _____ (*Mork & Mindy*)
21. Wilma _____ (*Buck Rogers in the 25th Century*)
22. Betty _____ (*The Flintstones*)
23. Doris_____ (*Green Acres*)
24. Aunt Esther _____ (*Sanford and Son*)
25. Paige _____ (*Ellen*)
26. Arnold _____ (*Diff'rent Strokes*)
27. Sally _____ (*The Dick Van Dyke Show*)
28. Jill _____ (*The Rookies*)
29. Robin _____ (*Magnum, P.I.*)
30. Billy _____ (*Melrose Place*)

31. Sam _____ (*Quantum Leap*)
32. Edna _____ (*The Simpsons*)
33. Roseanne _____ (*Roseanne*)
34. Diane _____ (*Cheers*)
35. Jenny _____ (*Happy Days*)
36. Chester _____ (*Soap*)
37. Joan _____ (*Please Don't Eat the Daisies*)
38. Danny _____ (*Full House*)
39. C.J. _____ (*West Wing*)
40. Captain Daniel _____ (*The Ghost and Mrs. Muir*)
41. Gidget _____ (*Gidget*)
42. Dave _____(*Dave's World*)
43. Reuben _____ (*The Partridge Family*)
44. Nell _____ (*Gimme A Break*)
45. Thelma "Mama" _____ (Mama's Family)

Character Names—**Answers**

1. Pierce
2. Kramden
3. Smart
4. Tate
5. Duncan
6. Wayne
7. Mertz
8. Sprague
9. Bodine
10. Hartley
11. Rutherford
12. Solo
13. Collins Stoddard
14. Lindstrom
15. Cunningham
16. Findlay
17. Barbarino
18. Tripper
19. Grant
20. McConnell
21. Deering
22. Rubble
23. Ziffel
24. Anderson
25. Clark
26. Jackson
27. Rogers
28. Danko
29. Masters
30. Campbell
31. Beckett
32. Krabappel
33. Conner
34. Chambers
35. Piccalo
36. Tate

37. Nash
38. Tanner
39. Cregg
40. Gregg
41. Lawrence
42. Barry
43. Kincaid
44. Harper
45. Harper

Jobs

What did these characters do for a living?
1. Ward Cleaver (*Leave it to Beaver*)
2. Gabe Kotter (*Welcome Back, Kotter*)
3. Miss Kitty Russell (*Gunsmoke*)
4. Jack Tripper (*Three's Company*)
5. Flo Castleberry (*Alice*)
6. Thomas Magnum (*Magnum, P.I.*)
7. Dorothy Zbornak (*The Golden Girls*)
8. Christine Sullivan (*Night Court*)
9. Pepper Anderson (*Police Woman*)
10. Lou Grant (*Lou Grant*)
11. Animal (*Lou Grant*)
12. Rhoda (*Rhoda*)
13. Ralph Kramden (*The Honeymooners*)
14. Barbara "Batgirl" Gordon (*Batman*)
15. Monica Colby (*The Colbys*)
16. Lois Lane (*Adventures of Superman*)
17. Andy Travis (*WKRP in Cincinnati*)
18. Julie McCoy (*The Love Boat*)
19. Perry Mason (*Perry Mason*)
20. Larry Dallas (*Three's Company*)
21. Isaac Washington (*The Love Boat*)
22. Frank Poncherello (*CHiPs*)
23. Kelly Garrett (*Charlie's Angels*)
24. Tom Bradford (*Eight is Enough*)
25. Quincy (*Quincy*)
26. Jennifer Hart (*Hart to Hart*)
27. Tony Nelson (*I Dream of Jeannie*)
28. Jessica Fletcher (*Murder, She Wrote*)
29. Darrin Stevens (*Bewitched*)
30. Michael Steadman (*thirtysomething*)

31. Agnes DiPesto (*Moonlighting*)
32. Sidney Shorr (*Love, Sidney*)
33. Tom Corbett (*The Courtship of Eddie's Father*)
34. Bookman (*Good Times*)
35. Larry Alder (*Hello, Larry*)
36. Richard Kimble (*The Fugitive*)
37. Danny Tanner (*Full House*)
38. Ellen Morgan (*Ellen*)
39. Julia Baker (*Julia*)
40. Harry Orwell (*Harry-O*)
41. Colt Seavers (*The Fall Guy*)
42. Tony Micelli (*Who's the Boss?*)
43. Angela Bower (*Who's the Boss?*)
44. Edina Monsoon (*Absolutely Fabulous*)
45. Ken Reeves (*The White Shadow*)
46. Samantha "Sam" Russell (*My Sister Sam*)
47. Jason Seaver (*Growing Pains*)
48. Caroline Duffy (*Caroline in the City*)
49. Emily Hartley (*The Bob Newhart Show*)
50. Joey Tribbiani (*Friends*)

Jobs—Answers

1. Accountant
2. Teacher
3. Owner/operator, Long Branch Saloon
4. Chef
5. Waitress
6. Private investigator
7. Teacher
8. Lawyer
9. Policewoman
10. Newspaper editor
11. Photographer
12. Window dresser
13. Bus driver
14. Librarian
15. Lawyer
16. Reporter
17. Station manager
18. Cruise director
19. Attorney
20. Used-car salesman
21. Bartender
22. Highway patrolman
23. Private investigator
24. Newspaper columnist
25. Medical examiner
26. Author
27. Astronaut
28. Author
29. Advertising executive
30. Advertising executive
31. Receptionist
32. Commercial artist
33. Magazine publisher
34. Building superintendent
35. Radio call-in show host
36. Doctor

37. TV sportscaster
38. Bookstore manager
39. Nurse
40. Private investigator
41. Stuntman
42. Housekeeper
43. Advertising executive
44. PR executive
45. Basketball coach
46. Commercial photographer
47. Psychiatrist
48. Cartoonist
49. Teacher (later episodes: Vice Principal)
50. Actor

Locales

Where did the following shows take place?
1. *Happy Days*
2. *The Donna Reed Show*
3. *Buck Rogers in the 25th Century* (first season)
4. *The Golden Girls*
5. *Evening Shade*
6. *The Munsters*
7. *Batman*
8. *Adventures of Superman*
9. *Dennis the Menace*
10. *Full House*
11. *Maude*
12. *Newhart*
13. *The Lucy Show*
14. *Family*
15. *Medical Center*
16. *Little House on the Prairie*
17. *The Flintstones*
18. *Private Benjamin*
19. *Gunsmoke*
20. *Bonanza*
21. *Magnum, P.I.*
22. *The Farmer's Daughter*
23. *Father Dowling Mysteries*
24. *Father Knows Best*
25. *The Simpsons*
26. *Fraiser*
27. *Joanie Loves Chachi*
28. *Murder, She Wrote*
29. *Dark Shadows*
30. *The Days and Nights of Molly Dodd*

31. *Buffy the Vampire Slayer*
32. *Flo*
33. *Alice*
34. *Absolutely Fabulous*

Locales—Answers

1. Milwaukee, Wisconsin
2. Hilldale
3. New Chicago (later episodes: outer space)
4. Miami
5. Evening Shade, Arkansas
6. Mockingbird Heights
7. Gotham City
8. Metropolis
9. Hillsdale
10. San Francisco
11. Tuckahoe, New York
12. Norwich, Vermont
13. Danfield, Connecticut (later seasons: San Francisco)
14. Pasadena, California
15. Los Angeles
16. Walnut Grove, Minnesota
17. Bedrock
18. Fort Bradley, near Biloxi, Mississippi
19. Dodge City, Kansas
20. The Ponderosa Ranch, near Virginia City, Virginia
21. Hawaii
22. Washington, D.C.
23. Chicago
24. Springfield
25. Springfield
26. Seattle, Washington
27. Chicago
28. Cabot Cove, Maine
29. Collinsport, Maine
30. New York City
31. Sunnydale, California
32. Cowtown, Texas
33. Phoenix, Arizona
34. London

Networks

Name the networks on which the following series were first broadcast:
1. *M*A*S*H*
2. *Gomer Pyle, U.S.M.C.*
3. *The Flying Nun*
4. *Dallas*
5. *Knight Rider*
6. *Mork & Mindy*
7. *The Man from U.N.C.L.E.*
8. *Dynasty*
9. *I Love Lucy*
10. *The Incredible Hulk*
11. *Donny and Marie*
12. *Cheers*
13. *Saturday Night Live*
14. *Rowan & Martin's Laugh-In*
15. *Murphy Brown*
16. *The Sopranos*
17. *Sisters*
18. *60 Minutes*
19. *Hogan's Heroes*
20. *Hazel*
21. *Star Trek*
22. *Good Times*
23. *Hawaii Five-O*
24. *Medical Center*
25. *The Time Tunnel*
26. *Little House on the Prairie*
27. *The Flip Wilson Show*
28. *Magnum, P.I.*
29. *Adam 12*
30. *Battlestar Galactica*

31. *The Patty Duke Show*
32. *Too Close For Comfort*
33. *Queer As Folk* (U.S. version)
34. *The Addams Family*
35. *Flipper*
36. *The Munsters*
37. *Lassie*
38. *Room 222*
39. *227*
40. *Mod Squad*
41. *Simon & Simon*
42. *Doogie Howser, M.D.*
43. *Murphy Brown*
44. *Doctor Quinn, Medical Woman*
45. *Wings*
46. *Coach*
47. *Matlock*
48. *Ally McBeal*
49. *L.A. Law*
50. *The Fall Guy*

Networks—**Answers**

1. CBS
2. CBS
3. NBC
4. CBS
5. NBC
6. ABC
7. NBC
8. ABC
9. CBS
10. CBS
11. ABC
12. NBC
13. NBC
14. NBC
15. CBS
16. HBO
17. NBC
18. CBS
19. CBS
20. NBC
21. NBC
22. CBS
23. CBS
24. CBS
25. ABC
26. NBC
27. NBC
28. CBS
29. NBC
30. ABC
31. ABC
32. ABC
33. Showtime
34. ABC
35. NBC
36. CBS

37. CBS
38. ABC
39. NBC
40. ABC
41. CBS
42. ABC
43. CBS
44. CBS
45. NBC
46. ABC
47. NBC
48. FOX
49. NBC
50. ABC

Spin-Offs

Name the series that spawned these shows:
1. *Fish*
2. *Flo*
3. *The Ropers*
4. *Three's A Crowd*
5. *Xena: Warrior Princess*
6. *Mork & Mindy*
7. *Lou Grant*
8. *Gloria*
9. *Empty Nest*
10. *Laverne & Shirley*
11. *Good Times*
12. *Maude*
13. *Knots Landing*
14. *Rhoda*
15. *The Jeffersons*
16. *Tabitha*
17. *The Sanford Arms*
18. *The Bionic Woman*
19. *The Facts of Life*
20. *Grady*
21. *Galactica 1980*

Spin-Offs—Answers

1. *Barney Miller*
2. *Alice*
3. *Three's Company*
4. *Three's Company*
5. *Hercules: The Legendary Journeys*
6. *Happy Days*
7. *The Mary Tyler Moore Show*
8. *All in the Family*
9. *The Golden Girls*
10. *Happy Days*
11. *Maude*
12. *All in the Family*
13. *Dallas*
14. *The Mary Tyler Moore Show*
15. *All in the Family*
16. *Bewitched*
17. *Sanford and Son*
18. *The Six Million Dollar Man*
19. *Diff'rent Strokes*
20. *Sanford and Son*
21. *Battlestar Galactica*

Theme Songs

Name the theme songs for the following shows:
1. *The Mary Tyler Moore Show*
2. *The Lone Ranger*
3. *The Golden Girls*
4. *The Doris Day Show*
5. *Designing Women*
6. *The Courtship of Eddie's Father*
7. *Laverne & Shirley*
8. *The Fall Guy*
9. *All in the Family*
10. *Angie*
11. *The Greatest American Hero*
12. *Who's the Boss?*
13. *Growing Pains*
14. *China Beach*
15. *Grace Under Fire*
16. *The Partridge Family*
17. *Ally McBeal*
18. *The Greatest American Hero*
19. *Cheers*

Theme Songs—Answers

1. "Love is All Around"
2. "William Tell Overture"
3. "Thank You For Being a Friend"
4. "Whatever Will Be, Will Be (Que Sera Sera)"
5. "Georgia On My Mind"
6. "Best Friend"
7. "Making Our Dreams Come True"
8. "The Unknown Stuntman"
9. "Those Were the Days"
10. "Different Worlds"
11. "Angie"
12. "Brand New Life"
13. "As Long As We Got Each Other"
14. "Reflections"
15. "Lady Madonna"
16. "When We're Singin'" (later reworked and retitled "Come On, Get Happy")
17. "Searching My Soul"
18. "Believe it or Not"
19. "Where Everybody Knows Your Name"

About the Author

Television has influenced the life of writer Craig Hamrick since he was a small child growing up in Coffeyville, Kansas. As he watched 1970s programming, he felt a bit displaced, because the only show even remotely connected to his hometown was *Little House on the Prairie.* (One of Laura Ingalls' childhood homes is now a log cabin museum near Coffeyville.)

The adventures of reporter Billie Newman on *Lou Grant* inspired him to study journalism in high school and then at Kansas Sate University. Later, Molly's experiences on *Days and Nights of Molly Dodd* made New York City look like a fun and magical place, which influenced his decision to move to the Big Apple in 1994. Today he and his boyfriend, director Joe Salvatore, live a stone's throw from Brooklyn Heights, where Patty and Cathy cavorted on *The Patty Duke Show.*

Craig has interviewed many classic TV stars, including Carol Burnett, Kaye Ballard, Desi Arnaz Jr., Sada Thompson, Gordon Jump, and William Windom. He's written several books about TV, including *The Dark Shadows Collectibles Book* and *Big Lou,* the biography of *All My Children* star Louis Edmonds. The books he has edited include *I'd Rather Eat Than Act,* by classic TV veteran Diana Millay; and *Lucy: A to Z,* the Lucille Ball encyclopedia, by Michael Karol.

For more information, visit www.craighamrick.com.

0-595-31034-6

Made in United States
North Haven, CT
10 June 2022

20036477R00093